Practical Mantra Yoga

A Guidebook for Self-Realization

Rudra Shivananda

Alight Publications
2015

Practical Mantra Yoga

By Rudra Shivananda

First Edition Published in January 2015

Alight Publications
PO Box 277
Live Oak, CA 95953

http://www.alightbooks.com

Softback ISBN: 978-1-931833-43-1
Ebook ISBN: 978-1-931833-45-5

Printed in the United States of America

Pranama to
SatGuru Yogiraj Siddhanath
The Source of
Kripa & Vidya

Contents

Practical Mantra Yoga

Introduction

One of the great paths of liberation is by the practice of mantras or spiritually charged sonic patterns formed from the Sanskrit language. This is the path of Mantra Yoga.

The word mantram combines the root manas (mind) with tram (protection) so the literal meaning is mind-protection. The mind is subject to innumerable perturbations that constantly disturb and keep it from the stillness that can lead the soul to higher consciousness. The proper practice of a mantra will lead the soul to the realization of the Self.

Since the effectiveness of mantras depend on their vibrations, their correct pronunciation become very important. They can be practiced by chanting aloud or by repeating mentally – some of them are meant to be mentally repeated for the purpose of being internalized, while others give emphasis to external effects. Mantras have been known to promote self-healing, spiritual development, as well as beneficial effects on the world around us.

Mantras can be used as the only means of spiritual liberation or as part of an integrated yogic system. Most yogic paths utilize some form of mantra or another in their techniques.

The most basic mantra is Om which is known as the "pranava mantra," the source of all mantras. It is the humming sound of creation because it is the vibration of the universe and the sound uttered by the Divine Creatrix. More complex sound patterns utilize the sound of Om in their beginning. It is used as an address for divine power.

Om is the principal mantra given by the great sage and yogi Patanjali in his Yoga Sutras. It can be chanted aloud, whispered or repeated mentally. In higher yogic techniques, instead of repeating the sound, the student should listen and try to hear the sound within and without – forming a powerful connection with the Universal Soul.

Nowadays, the emphasis is on the mantras which utilize bija or seed sounds because of their easier pronunciation, and prevalent use in tantric systems. Mantras were originally conceived in the ancient scriptures known as the Vedas. When they are crafted into two-line verses, they are called "shlokas."

The following is from Rigveda X-191-4:

> *Samaani va aakutih*
> *samaanaa hrdayaani vah.*
> *Samaanamastu vo mano*
> *yathaa vah susahaasati.*

> Let us unite our intentions.
> May your hearts also be in unison.
> United be the thoughts of all,
> That we may all happily agree.

The repetition of this mantra tends to promote a team consciousness and help a group to achieve common goals. It is very helpful to chant in a group.

My focus going forward is to introduce a practical guidebook to a spiritual mantra practice that will be effective to take the aspriant to higher consciousness. There is no pre-requisite for the practice in Part 1 and everyone can benefit from the mantras there. The mantra practice in Part 2 is compariitively complex and will require strong concentration. Although I've included advanced mantras in part 3 aimed at Self-Realization, it is must be emphasized that initiation into the appropriate mantra and its practice is necessary to fully realize its power.

What is a mantra?

*A quick introductory tour since mantra
means many different things to various people*

A sound, a syllable, word or group of words that are considered
capable transforming either the external environment or the
internal consciousness or both

A subtle sound vibration that when repeated will
expand one's awareness or consciousness

A mystical formula in Sanskrit that may be
recited or sung in a special manner to obtain a result

Chanting of a mantra gives the power to heal

Chanting a mantra can harm and destroy

Chanting of a mantra gives protection against evil and harm

Chanting of a mantra confers supernatural powers

Chanting a mantra leads to blissful states

Chanting a mantra leads to
liberation from the cycle of birth and death

A mantra is a bridge between normal consciousness and
super-consciousness

The effect of a mantra
depends on its vibration and not its meaning

The most powerful mantras are
protected from misuse by being locked with passwords

A Mantra most often invoke the power of
some apsect of universal forces

The mantra protects the mind from the ego

The mantra protects the soul from the mind

The mantra leads the soul to the buddhi or higher mind

The mantra leads the soul past the buddhi to the True Self

Basic Mantra Knowledge

The Key Parts of Mantra

Now, let us begin our study of the science of mantra by looking at the components that constitute all mantras.

Remember that for classifying mantras, we can consider that there are two primary reasons to chant mantras - to fulfill our ego-desires or for Self-realization. Some mantras can be used for both purposes such as the mahamritunajaya mantra for preventing untimely death as well as for liberation from the cycle of karmic suffering.

Every mantra has six parts (shadanga): rishi, chandas, devatha, beejam, keelakam and shakti. Knowing the six parts for the specific mantra we are following is critical for achieving the benefits in a timely manner. It is not always possible to know all the six parts and sometimes it is not necessary but in all cases, the benefits can still be attained albeit in a slower pace through intense and regular practice.

Rishi identifies the sage who discovered the mantra first – that is, he is the seer of the mantra such as Vishwamitra for the Gayatri mantra. In the case of some tantric mantras, the rishi is the first one who attained perfection or siddhi in that mantra. In either case, the initial life force of the mantra comes from the kundalini

[6]

shakti of the rishi. It is necessary to connect with the rishi if one is seriously going to undertake the practice of a mantra.

Chandas includes the proper pronunciation of that mantra as well as in some cases the proper manner or melody that accompanies its chanting. The pronunciation is critical for all mantras as the sound patterns form the body of the universal energy that is being invoked by the mantra and a badly formed body will not be a suitable vehicle to carry the energy needed. The melody is more important in the case of mantras designed for satisfying desires as these require an additional instrument to give external effects. The melody is absent or less important in the case of liberation mantras recited primarily in the mind.

Devatha is the aspect of the universal power that will give the benefits for that mantra. Generally for each mantra there will be an inherent deity (adhisthan devatha) with specific meditative form (dhyana rupa). There may also be a separate meditative mantra called dhyana sloka that can be learned to supplement the main mantra. Also, a mantra may have several deities and it needs the direction from the initiator to correctly point to the right one for the student. An example is the Gayatri which is said to have three deities – Gayatri, Savitri and Saraswati.

Beejam (Bijam is a variant spelling) is the seed from which the mantra is formed and gives the basic character (tattva) of the mantra - soft (jala tattva) or hard (agni tatva). There are some single-syllable or one-word mantras that encapsulate the seed and are called beeja mantras.

Keelakam is the key to open the lock to get results. Most of the powerful mantras are locked and require a key to open. Some mantras such as Om or Nama Shivaya are unlocked and can practiced without the keelakam, but others are closely locked with hidden keys such as the Gayatri. The keelakam can be another mantra or sloka or can be the transference of a particular touch or energy during the initiation by the mantra siddha.

Shakti is the power of mantra. This is the power we get from perfecting the mantra.

Besides these six parts of the mantra, there are three supplementary parts that are only present for some mantras - **sankalpam, kavacham and ardham**.

Sankalpam is the intent for the mantra practice – it incorporates the will-power of the practitioner and announces to the universe the results desired. If the sankalpam is moksha, then it is not necessary to repeat it every time but if the goal is a material desire, then it necessary to continually remind oneself the reason for the practice.

Some mantras attract obstructions to those who try to practice them and so a protective armor is necessary – this is the kavacham that needs to be recited before commencing the primary mantra.

Ardham is the meaning of that mantra – this is mostly of subsidiary importance and even absent in the case of beeja mantras but play an important role in meditative slokas for deities. In some mantras, the key is the devotional fervor of the seeker.

It is important for a student to receive the proper guidance when undertaking the practice of a mantra – the critical elements should be identified and incorporated into the mantra yoga sadhana.

Know the function of a mantra

Most of the time, spiritual seekers acquire mantras without understanding their specific power or function. Sometimes, it is because a friend has talked about it or often because it is mentioned in some inspirational book or their desires lead them to ask their teachers for one.

Even when the name of the mantra gives some indication of the direction of its power, it will be foolish to undertake a mantra practice without a specific instruction about its effects. There are many Durga and Ganesha mantras and their effects are all different and not interchangeable

There is an assumption by sincere seekers that there cannot be harm in repeating a spiritual or healing mantra and that the worst that can happen is simply that nothing will happen. This is foolish - it is like playing with dynamite - something is bound to happen. This is especially true when students ask their teachers to give them a mantra without the prerequisite precautions and wisdom to discern the possible effects. Both the teacher and the student will suffer from the karmic backlash.

Another false assumption is that a mantra will have the same or at least similar effect on everyone - this is not true due to the fact that everyone has a different karmic constitution and resonates differently to the vibratory effects of a mantra. There can be an allergic reaction for some! The really powerful mantras are able to overcome the karmic variations and perform their functions. However, even in such cases, there can be negative side-effects.

It is important therefore to be very sure about the effects of a mantra in general and also specifically for the practitioner before embarking on a practice. The various sources that can provide the relevant information are:

- From the spiritual teacher who is authorized as well as energized to be able to give the mantra. If the teacher doesn't know and/or cannot discern the individual effects, then he should admit it and desist from giving mantras. It should not be expected that every spiritual teacher is a mantra master.

- From a spiritual lineage - often a particular school of yoga will have a set of mantras that are to be recited by all its members. These generally invoke lineage of masters or specific divine powers that protect or help the students of the lineage.

- From authoritative written sources - there are many sources giving the instructions on Vedic, puranic or tantric mantras but these should be carefully examined for their authenticity and accuracy.

- From astrological calculation - the choice, effects and manner of practice of many healing as well spiritual mantras can be determined be delineating the students Vedic horoscope and a knowledge of the astrological remedies.

- From personal experience - this can be possible for very advanced yogis who have attained higher level of consciousness and have made a serious practice of mantra vidya.

Just doing a mantra and hoping for the best is not a recommended solution to the ignorance of its possible karmic consequences. It is important to be sure of one's motives before embarking on a mantra practice. Ask for the appropriate mantra to serve the desitred purpose from an authorized and reputable source and follow instruction completely.

The Power Of Mantra

It is said that a mantra possesses power to transform, manifest, destroy or protect depending on its purpose. Where does this power come from?

A mantra is dormant or in seed form until it is first born from being drawn into the universe by the power or shakti of a rishi (a yogi who is also a "seer" of a mantra.) The seers of vedic mantras are usually known and should be invoked before the repetition of the mantras. These would include the famous mantras such as the Gayatri from Vishvamitra and the Mahamryutanjaya from Markandeya. The rishi has instilled his own shakti energy into the mantra in order to give it life and so the power of the mantra initially derives from the seer. This model is distinct from that in which the mantra has always existed and the seer in a raised consciousness plays a passive role of "seeing the mantra." There are also mantras in the puranas and some of them are attributed to a rishi also, such as the puranic mrutanjaya mantra from Kakbushandh. It is instructive to know that some of the major vedic or puranic mantras have some story associated with their genesis as well.

Tantric mantras are shrouded in mystery and there is generally less information about their antecedents, since until recent times they were transmitted secretly from Master to disciple only, but the principle still holds that the Master who created the mantra in the first place must have breathed his awakened kundalini life-force into the mantra itself.

Therefore the foundation power of the mantra depends on its originator.

As time goes by and more and more people repeat the mantra, it grows in power, just as a person acquires life-force in growing up while eating and breathing. However, the basic power is still dependent on the foundation power of the rishi just as a person is born with a certain amount of birth prana.

When someone is initiated into a mantra, the initiator must also infuse his kundalini shakti into it for the disciple to benefit from it. The initiator himself must have access to the foundation power of the mantra through another Master and so on up the chain of transmission and has subsequently realized its true essence. The disciple in the beginning is drawing on the initiation power and slowly coming to realize the foundation power over a period of time. Only when the disciple has realized the foundation power of the mantra is he a master of it.

The initiation power helps to jumpstart the student's access to the mantra.

If the student uses up the initiation power and has not connected with the foundation power, then the mantra is dead within him and he will need to be re-initiated.

Why am I talking about this? It is important to understand where a mantra comes from and its originator if possible. Mantras cannot be created by just anyone. There is a misconception that someone in a heightened awareness can make up some syllables that appeal to him and it's a mantra – that is simply not true. Such "mantras" may have some feel-good effect just as any well-written jingle, popular song or poem can have, but cannot have the transformative power of a true mantra because it would lack the foundation power of the awakened kundalini.

Secondly, only one who has internalized and gained accessed to the foundation power as well as have his kundalini shakti awakened can initiate another person into the mantra. Being initiated into a mantra by a well-meaning teacher is not sufficient to ensure the promised benefit. It is a misconception that anyone can initiate into a mantra if they have learned it, can pronounce it or have repeated it a certain number of times.

Understanding Our Subtle Nature

In order to understand how mantras work and the process of mantra yoga, we need to learn more about our subtle nature – our possession of a series of subtle bodies that give expression to our phenomenal being and the energetic centers within our subtle bodies which are responsible for our physical, energetic, emotional and mental nature.

The Five-Body Existential Model

Refer to Figure 1.

1. The physical body is what most of us identify with. It is the only reality which the majority of humanity recognizes, being composed of blood and bones, the nervous system and sense organs
2. The energy body is just above our normal conscious perception, but can be sensed in recognition of the presence of vitality. It is like an overlay on the physical body energizing and regulating the physical cells. It acts as a channel between the physical world and the higher subtle worlds. Here is where the *chakras* or energy centers are particularly active.
3. The emotional body serves as the mediation between the physical and mental bodies, converting the physical

vibrations from the neutral sensations into the "emotionally charged sensations" by adding the qualities of "pleasant" or "unpleasant" or encapsulating it with feelings such as desire or fear. Most physical diseases arise from the emotional or energy bodies.

4. The mental body is the abode of knowledge and analytical thinking. The "emotionally charged sensations" from the emotional body is processed into perceptual units and fitted into patterns calling forth responses which vibrate back through the emotional body back into the physical realm, causing a physical reaction. This is the realm of thoughts and habit patterns.

5. The causal body is both the home of wisdom and of our *karmic* debts. This is the abode of the evolving soul. Higher abstract and intuitive insights arise from here.

The five-body complex exists and functions in different "dimensions" and each is maintained by a different type of energy, from the physical chemical reactions to the subtlest consciousness energy. Each of the bodies have their own energy centers or chakras as well as energy channels for controlling and distributing of their own level of energy. Orthodox science only recognizes the centers and channels associated with the physical body, where the cardio-vascular system represents the channels, and the brain and various nerve plexuses correspond to the energy centers. As the *chakras* are activated and awakened, you will become aware of the corresponding dimension of reality, giving you a fuller understanding of the lower dimensions.

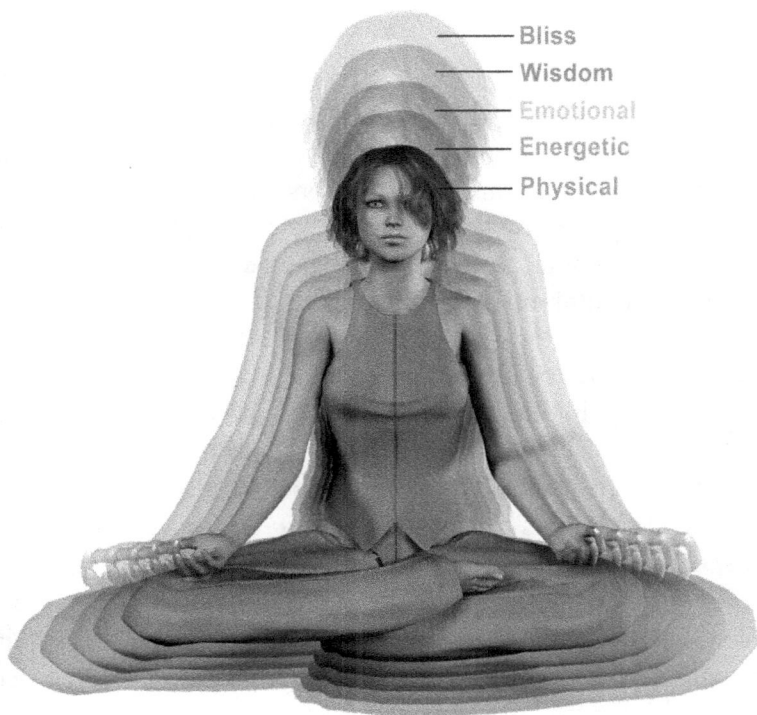

Figure 1
The Five Body Model

A Simple Chakra Model

Refer Figure 2

It has been pointed out in ancient yogic texts, that yogis are those who truly know the *Chakras* or Energy Centers. This exemplifies how critical and potentially complex this whole topic can become. Not only are these centers important for spiritual techniques, they are also essential for the healing and well-being of our physical bodies, energetic imbalances, emotional bombs and negative mental modifications.

We need not delve too deeply into their functions and structures as we are only interested in the effect of mantras on them. However, it is necessary to know that these energy centers can be modelled with a set number of lotus petals and in each center, the associated "deities", the magical *mantras* or key derivative sounds, or the many other correspondences can have an effect.

The detailed description of the chakras are necessary for certain tantric paths and for Kundalini Yoga. They are best learned through a reliable teacher, and not through books. As an example, the key sounds or mantras need to be pronounced correctly to have the right effect, and also, an energy transmission needs to accompany the imparting of the sound to provide the impetus towards the desired effect. The only Sound that can be worked with in the chakras without initiation is the Sound of *OM*, which is the Universal Mantra given to all of humanity for our evolution.

These Energy Centers cannot be found by dissecting the physical body, but only through achieving higher states of consciousness.

Figure 2 gives the location of the *chakras* in relation to the physical body. They are called wheels because of the circular movement of the energies that whirl in and out of them. For some techniques, they are visutalized as balls of light.

These Energy Centers are affected by changes in our internal states, as well as by external vibrations, such as thoughts, words, or actions of others. In the average person, these Centers are functioning sub-optimally, and are not harmonized with each other. As the health of the person is decreased through pollution and tension, the more out of tune these Centers become. Many Self-healing exercises serve as means of harmonizing these imbalanced Energy Centers.

Center 1: This is also called the Root Center, and is located at the base of the spine in the perineum and is the root and support of all the other centers. It is connected with the subtle element "earth" representing solidity, and therefore is closely related to the physical body. It is visualized as a lotus with four petals.

Center 2: The sacral center is located two inches above the 1st Center along the spine, and is associated with the subtle element water, representing fluidity and movement. This is the center for the emotional body. It is visualized as a lotus with six petals.

Center 3: The navel center is located at the level of the navel, and is associated with the subtle element fire, representing transformation of energy. This center is closely related to the energy body. It is visualized as a lotus with ten petals.
Center 4: The heart center is located at the spine at the heart level and is associated with the subtle element air, representing the mind and is the center of the mental body. It is visualized as a lotus with twelve petals.

Center 5: The throat center is located at the throat and is associated with the subtle element ether, representing consciousness. This is the center for the causal or spiritual body, and is considered the seat of the soul. It is visualized as a lotus with sixteen petals.

Center 6: The third-eye center is located in the center of the head at the level just above the eyes, traditionally called the "third eye" and is the center for super-consciousness. It is visualized as a lotus with two petals.

Center 7: this is located at the crown of the head and is associated with the Absolute or Transcendent Reality.

When the first six chakras are tuned and balanced and finally, fully awakened, they will open our consciousness to the Divine Reality of the seventh Center.

It is known that there are billions of chakras or energy centers in the energy body, just as therre are billions of cells in the physical body. Howevver, for spiritual purposes, we are only interested in the primary seven chakras along the spiritual spine that overlays the physical spine.

The chakras are energy vibrations. Each chakra vibrates to certain frequencies. **The ancient yogis found that certain sounds affected certain centers more and formulated the fifty letters of the Sanskrit alphablet to correspond to the fifty petals of the first six chakras**. Refer to figure 3. This can help to explain how mantras work because they affect the pranic centers and in turn the physical, emotional and mental bodies.

This teaching has profound ramifications for understanding the human spiritual physiology and the mechanics of what happens when we chant Sanskrit mantras and hymns.

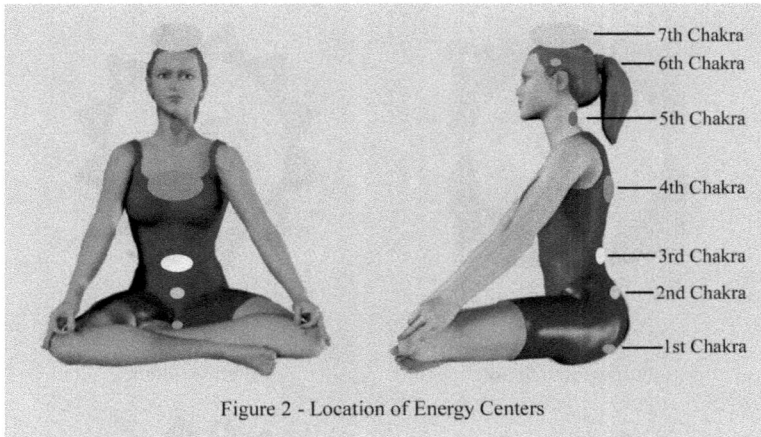

Figure 2 - Location of Energy Centers

The Kriya Yogi, Paramhansa Yogananda has written that, "In a highly simplified description, it may be said that the fifty letters or sounds of the Sanskrit alphabet are on the petals of the sahasrara, and that each alphabetical vibration in turn is connected with a specific petal on the lotuses in the spinal centers (which have a total of fifty corresponding petals...) 'Petals' mean ray or vibrations. These vibrations, ... are responsible for various psychological and physiological activities in the physical and astral bodies of man."

Another correspondence found by the yogis was that certain parts of the physical body felt the effect of different sounds and formulated a useful healing model based on this theory that is called the mantra purusha. We will not be working more with this model since its effects are more on the physical body but this re-inforces the power of the sounds in the Sanskrit alphabet.Refer to figures 4 and 5.

In the next section, we will look at the scientific corroboration for the effects of sound on our emotions and mind.

Muladhara Chakra

Anahata Chakra

Svadhisthana Chakra

Vishuddha Chakra

Manipura Chakra

Ajna Chakra

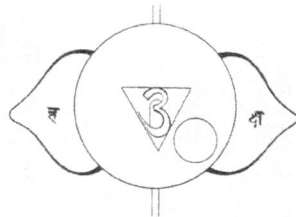

Figure 3

Chakras and the Sanskrit letters

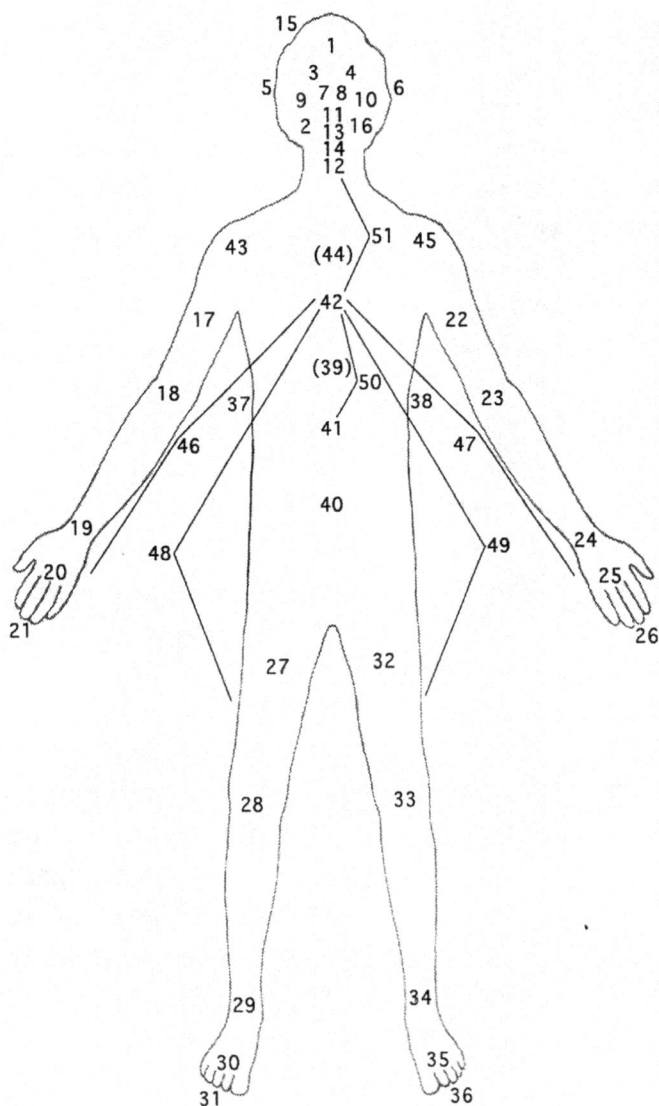

Figure 4

The Mantra Purusha

1.	अ	a	forehead	27.	ट	ṭ	right thigh
2.	आ	ā	face	28.	ठ	ṭh	right knee
3.	इ	i	right eye	29.	ड	ḍ	right ankle
4.	ई	ī	left eye	30.	ढ	ḍh	right metatarsals
5.	उ	u	right ear	31.	ण	ṇ	right toe tips
6.	ऊ	ū	left ear	32.	त	t	left thigh
7.	ऋ	ṛ	right nostril	33.	थ	th	left knee
8.	ॠ	ṝ	left nostril	34.	द	d	left ankle
9.	ऌ	ḷ	right cheek	35.	ध	dh	left metatarsals
10.	ॡ	ḹ	left cheek	36.	न	n	right toe tips
11.	ए	e	upper lip	37.	प	p	whole right side
12.	ऐ	ai	lower lip	38.	फ	ph	left side
13.	ओ	o	upper teeth	39.	ब	b	back
14.	औ	au	lower teeth	40.	भ	bh	navel
15.	अं	aṃ	head	41.	म	m	stomach area
16.	अः	aḥ	mouth	42.	य	y	heart
17.	क	k	right upper arm	43.	र	r	right shoulder
18.	ख	kh	right elbow	44.	ल	l	center upper back
19.	ग	g	right wrist	45.	व	v	left shoulder
20.	घ	gh	right knuckles	46.	श	ś	heart to right hand
21.	ङ	ṅ	right finger tips	47.	ष	ṣ	heart to left hand
22.	च	c	left upper arm	48.	स	s	heart to right leg
23.	छ	ch	left elbow	49.	ह	h	heart to left leg
24.	ज	j	left wrist	50.	ळ	rh	heart to stomach
25.	झ	jh	left knuckles	51.	क्ष	kṣ	heart to mouth
26.	ञ	ñ	left finger tips				

Figure 5

The letters Corresponding to Mantra Purusha

How do Mantras Work?

A Scientific Approach

Spoken mantras are audible sound vibrations. Sound vibrations have been shown to have visible physical effects – experiments with tuning forks and vibrating strings can cause specific patterns in small particles. It is a common experience that sounds can effect emotions in human beings and animals – we can all testify to the way certain music affect our moods.

Music has also been shown to have an effect on the health and growth of plants. A recent study [October 2014] published in the Journal of International Environmental Science and Development by V Chivukula and S Ramaswamy concluded that:

> Music influences the growth of plants and can either promote or restrict the growth of plants (depending on the type of music being played). The present experiment is aimed to study the effect of music on 30 Rose (Rosa chinensis) plants taken in separate pots. The plants were divided into five groups and each group was subjected to one of the following types of music, Indian Classical music, Vedic chants, Western Classical music, and Rock music while one group was kept in silence as the control group. The elongation of shoot, internode elongation, the number of flowers and the diameter of the flowers were recorded and changed studied over a period of 60 days.

> Significant differences have been noted. It was seen that the plants

exposed to Vedic chants showed the maximum elongation of shoot, maximum number of flowers and highest diameter of flowers. The internode elongation was highest in plants exposed to Indian classical music. This clearly shows that the subjecting the plants to Vedic chants or Indian classical music promotes the growth of plants as compared to the control group or subjecting them to Western classical or rock music.

There is no consensus on a scientific basis for this kind of experimental data. It is not my intention to get into the scientific controversies surrounding such experiments. However, it is interesting because such studies confirm our own experiences that mantras somehow have an effect on us.

Now, of greater interest are the experiments on water crystals by Masaru Emoto because the mantras that we are most interested in for yoga are repeated silently and not aloud. Therefore, we cannot invoke the effect of sound but must go deeper into whether thoughts can have an effect on matter!

The experiments of Masaru Emoto on water crystals and consciousness have been visually documented on the web. He freezes droplets of water and then examines them under a dark field microscope that has photographic capabilities to show the molecular changes that can be observed.

Some examples from his works include:

- Water from clear mountain springs and streams had beautifully formed crystalline structures, while the crystals of polluted or stagnant water were deformed and distorted. Distilled water exposed to classical music took delicate, symmetrical crystalline shapes.

- When the words "thank you" were taped to a bottle of distilled water, the frozen crystals had a similar shape to the crystals formed by water that had been exposed to Bach's "Goldberg Variations"- music composed out of gratitude to the man it was named for.

- When water samples were bombarded with heavy metal music or labeled with negative words, or **when negative thoughts and emotions were focused intentionally upon them, such as "Adolf Hitler", the water did not form crystals at all and displayed chaotic, fragmented structures.**

- When water was treated with aromatic floral oils, the water crystals tended to mimic the shape of the original flower.

Let us not forget that our own bodies at birth are more than sixty percent water and remain high throughout life (depending upon weight and body type) and that the earth's surface is more than sixty percent water as well. The work of Mr. Emoto have shown us that water is far from inanimate, but is actually alive and responsive to our every thought and emotion. Perhaps, having seen this, we can begin to really understand the awesome power that we possess, through choosing our thoughts and intentions, to heal ourselves and the earth. A little thought will help us understand that disbelief in the power of our thoughts can itself have a strong effect on the outcome of what we are trying to achieve.

Each of us has the capability to think positive thoughts and fill our lives and the world around us with the effect of these positive thoughts. The sages have always taught that the external world is a reflection of our own inner world of thoughts and emotions. This has been demonstrated by the effect of consciousness on water crystals – how amazing.

It has also been demonstrated in a double-blind study that ultrasound probes applied to the skull can improve subjective mood, and it has been evidenced that even imagining performing musical exercises rewires and strengthens nerve connections.

Both of these studies speak to the capacity of mental recitation of mantra to activate and affect the physical nervous system.

The power of sounds and thoughts to affect us and cause changes to our minds and consciousness is not just due to the fact that our body has water as a major constituent. According to the yogis and sages of India, we have subtle bodies that contain structures called chakras that are energy centers. We introduced these energy in an earlier section of the book. However, at this time, we only need to understand that these energy centers absorb, store and distribute life-force energy or prana to all parts of our physical, emotional and mental systems. These chakras vibrate with certain energetic frequencies which are affected by the vibrations of the sounds and thoughts. The sages developed the ancient Sanskrit alphabet to resonate with the frequencies of the chakras. This means that mantras formed from the Sanskrit letters will have known effects on specific energy centers and their corresponding physical organs, as well as, emotional and mental states.

Figure X shows the chakras with their corresponding Sanskrit letters. As you can see, the throat chakra resonates to the 16 vowels as well as a central sound called the seed or bija sound. Each of the major six chakras has a central seed sound in addition to the Sanskrit letters.

Studies on the effects of Mantras

There have also been studies on specific mantras that claim significant physiological and mental changes resulting from their repetition. It is worthwhile considering them even though much of it is carried out by believers and therefore somewhat suspect in the mainstream scientific community.

The Sound of Om

The mystic OM does not have a translation. It is called the "birthing hum of the universe", since according to the sages, every atom and being in the universe is vibrating with some harmonic of this sound. It is also the sound that gave birth to the universe – what is called "The Word of God." In the scriptures of ancient India, OM is considered as the most powerful of all the mantras. The others are considered aspects of OM, and OM is the matrix of all other mantras. The syllable OM is quite familiar to Indians, since it occurs in every prayer. Invocation to most gods begins with this syllable OM which is also pronounced as AUM. The syllable OM is not specific to Indian culture. It has religious significance in other religions also. OM is not given any specific definition and is considered to be a cosmic sound, a primordial sound and even the totality of all sounds. In the West, this Indian tradition of beginning all names of the Divine with Om seems to have a counterpart in the use of the words that describe God – **Om**nipresent, **Om**nipotent or **Om**niscience. It is amen and amin, as well as the alpha and the omega.

Chanting OM resulted in significant brain wave frequency changes, as evidenced in the subject's EEG readings. Gujare, Ladhake, and Thakare from Spina's college of Enginering & Technology in Maharashtra, India, explain the reading in this way, "From this we could conclude that chanting OM mantra results in stabilization of [the] brain, removal of worldly thoughts and an increase of energy. It means that concentrating on OM mantra and continuously doing it slowly shifts our attention. It is a reflection of the most fundamental interlocking processes in our bodies…the harmony we play echoes the harmonic relationships of every vital system i.e. our heartbeat, our breathing, our brainwaves pulsing, our neuronal firing, our cells throbbing, our metabolic, enzymatic, and hormonal rhythms and our behaviors in our addictions and our habits. In this sense OM mantra is a brain stabilizer, by practicing it one can enter deeper and deeper into a natural state, which is also an energy medicine for human beings under stress."

Bija Mantras

There have been studies on root syllables (sounds that have no correspondence in the physical world), that seem to show that they can enhance certain states of mind. The sound "m" for example, resonates with the right brain. Most of us are quite left-brain dominant in the West, which means our intuition, or emotions, and our non-linear thinking is often less pronounced than the logical and analytical modes induced by a predominant left brain. Bija mantras can be very helpful in balancing the brain hemispheres as well as the chakra system.

Mantra and Neuroscience

Recent investigations in neuroscience seem to support the ancient science of sound in yoga used for increasing awareness and expanding emotional states of the human personality.

There have been studies that suggest mantra may regulate certain circuits in the body, among them: neural circuits, cellular signaling circuits, gene regulating circuits, biometric circuits, as well as activating dormant circuits to speed up our psycho-spiritual evolution. Some neuroscientists believe that mantra is the evolutionary tool that can rewire humanity to higher consciousness.

Neuroscientists have posited that the major phonemes of speech have evolved to resemble the sounds from the external environment in kinds of interactive and sequential events – a primitive form of onomatopoeia, where the sounds of the words resemble the events themselves, such as in "screech" and "crash." This would indicate that speech, and even music can be considered ordered sound narratives that make use of our brain's evolved capacity to perceive natural sounds.

It is interesting that sounds themselves, before they are assigned meaning, may be felt to resonate in different parts of the body and mind, creating actual interactions or events. In the yogic point of view, mantras are information, in the literal sense of in-forming: the creation of form, or interactions. The ancients believed that the Sanskrit language has a divine orgina and has mystical power. In the scientific term, we can say that it is an information sequencing system that mimics the process of nature's repeating patterns. A modern Sanskrit scholar Dr. Douglas Brooks has said, "Sanskrit tells us what Nature shows us. A limited number of rules give an arbitrarily large number of outcomes. The way Nature goes about its business, Sanskrit goes about its language." Just like the experience of immersing oneself in music evokes certain emotions and mental states, mantra uses sound to evoke movement of physical and emotional energy through stimulation of the nervous system, from which emerges meaning and narrative.

In order to have insight into and validate a mantra for ourselves, it must be experienced and felt through introspection. Let's take the mantra Om, or Aum which we've already examined previously. If Aum is indeed onomatopoeic, then performing it can create an event inside the nervous system, which can then become an object of concentration and meditation, and thereby a focal point for expanding physical and emotional awareness.

In linguistic terms, Aum does not have any plosives or fricatives, only sonorants – so that would mean that it does not correspond to any type of solid-object physical events that the brain was evolved to perceive. A, U and M are sonorants and so qualifies an object that inherently has no interactions – in physical terms, it represents a formless object. Experiment with resonating the mantra aloud or even whispering it, allowing air to flow through the nasal passage, smoothly transitioning between the three sounds. The A (as in "car") can feel like a wide opening and has a broader vibratory effect on the physical body, corresponding to the consciousness of the waking state. The U (as in "soup"), has a funneling effect, narrowing the consciousness into subtler sensations such as thoughts and impressions, approximating the dream state. The nasal M sound is like the drone of a bee; it makes the cranium vibrate in the cerebral cortex, corresponding to the dreamless sleep state.

The above experiential treatment of Aum is closely matched by the yogic teachings that it represents and has the capacity to progressively open up the practitioner to the ever-present formless and timeless reality.

Mantra and Cymatics

The founder of Cymatics, Hans Jenny put sand, dust and fluids on a metal plate connected to an oscillator which could produce a broad spectrum of frequencies. The sand or other substances were organized into different structures characterized by geometric shapes typical of the frequency of the vibration emitted by the oscillator.

Jenny using lycopodium powder and imposing a vocalization of the mantra Om was able to form a circle with a center point – consistent with one of the yogic images of Om! Using different frequencies, structures that looked like mandalas or natural forms too shape. He felt that they were formed by the vibrational energy of an invisible force field all around us.

Although cymatics is considered a pseudoscience, it does seem to indicate a connection between sound and natural form.

It has long been held that the Sanskrit language is code for the patterns of nature, sonic representations of the way nature works. Therefore mantras in Sanskrit hold within them the latent forms of the universe. As these latent forms are manifested from stillness and subtle vibrations becoming audible sound, they have the capacity to shape reality.

Mantra — Effects on Stress and Depression

A 3-group study was made on the effects of chanting the "Hare Krishna Maha-mantra" on stress, depression, and the three modes of nature - sattva, rajas, and tamas, often described as the basis for human psychology. Sixty-two subjects, self-selected through newspaper advertisements in a Southeastern university town, completed the study. The subjects had an average age was 24 years, with 31 males and 31 females participating. Stress was measured with the Index of Clinical Stress, depression was measured with the Generalized Contentment Scale, and the modes of nature, or gunas, were measured with the Vedic Personality Inventory. Participants were randomly assigned to a maha mantra group, an alternate mantra (made-up by the researcher) group, and a control group. Subjects in each of the chanting groups chanted their mantra approximately 25 minutes each day.

The primary hypotheses of the study were based on Vedic theory, and stated that the maha mantra group would increase sattva, and decrease stress, depression – this was shown to be the case beyond statistical probability as compared to the other two groups.

The Barrier to Effective Mantra Yoga

Mantra Yoga is that discipline by means of which one can attain Self-realization through the repetition of sounds or words that bridge the gap between our normal consciousness and super-conscious states of awareness. It said to be a powerful and effective means especially during the eras when the average human consciousness is gravitating towards the lower levels of materiality. Mantras are also used as part of other yogic methodologies such as kriya yoga, raja yoga and bhakti yoga as well as in devotional practices such as ritual pujas and all types of tantric techniques.

However, I've often heard from practitioners who have been initiated into one or more mantras that even after many years of repetition (some tell me that they've been repeating their mantras for twenty years), they have not received the spiritual breakthrough promised. At the beginning, there occurs some encouraging signs such as less tension and more mental focus and maybe even visions but after some time, they are discouraged - their teachers tell them to be patient and keep practicing. Most spiritual seekers give up after a few years while others repeat their mantra sporadically as a security blanket or out of habit, hoping something will happen.

It is of course important to have patience and persevere in any spiritual discipline but the barrier to effective mantra yoga is more fundamental then the modern tendency towards the quick-fix and immediate gratification of desires. We have a desire to become Self-realized and we think that by getting initiated into a mantra will be an easy and quick method because that is what is promised in many cases. The fundamental barrier is the lack of preparation in the modern spiritual seeker.

The mantra works like a seed in the mind and by proper cultivation, it will grow as a spiritual tree that can bridge the gap between lower and higher consciousness as a physical tree has its roots in the earth and its branches in the sky. The spiritual tree has its roots in the higher consciousness and its branches in the lower. The seed cannot grow if the ground is not properly prepared or it might grow a little and wither away after some time, even if it is properly watered. The ground that has to be prepared for the mantra is the mind itself.

There are different consciousness levels for mantras – they come down from and can lead back to different levels of super-consciousness. The modern tendency is for teachers to give students higher levels of mantras, especially tantric or vedic ones which cannot grow due to the inherent unpreparedness of the student's mind. The normal mind is full of confusion and myriad thought patterns due to our karmic dispositions and is not a suitable ground for higher mantras. It would be like giving a physics book to a child in kindergarten. The students are demanding higher mantras because they have read or heard about them but what is missing is the proper means. Even teachers have forgotten or do not know what the proper sequence of mantra yoga should be taught.

Traditionally, the student is prepared first with mantras that can remove some of the minor disturbances of the mind – these mantras were taught to children and they repeated them every day. Prior to puberty, the student is then given a mantra sadhana or practice which involves a higher level of awareness and concentration. This second level of mantra sadhana would be practiced for a few years or longer depending on the aspirations of youth - whether towards more spiritual pursuits or towards the

[34]

house-holder duties. However, should the student at some time in life have the desire and opportunity to receive initiation into the higher mantras, his or her mind would be well-prepared and there would be rapid progress and results.

The issue is that in our times, the preparation phases have been neglected by the rapid modernization of India and the increasing demand for spiritual fixes in the West, leading to the degeneration of the effectiveness of mantra yoga. There are many unqualified teachers who are forced to give initiations to satisfy their students and even Masters have had to lower their standards to cater for the demands of the spiritual seekers. It is more difficult to find a good student than to find a good teacher these days!

It is necessary to put back the step-by-step structure into mantra yoga and not promulgate misleading and unrealistic expectations from a single mantra initiation for the unprepared. It is important to understand that even if one has the good karma to receive an initiation, if one has not made the effort to prepare one-self, the fruits of the initiation may not appear in this life. However, be of good cheer, because any sincere practice will have a positive effect sooner or later and no effort is wasted.

A Progressive Mantra Yoga Program

The obstacles to an effective or successful mantra yoga practice that can lead to Self-realization in one life-time are:

1. Unpreparedness of the student whose mind is not trained

2. A qualified teacher who can give the mantra (s)

3. Getting a right mantra at the right time – this is particularly neglected because there is an assumption that a mantra that works well with one person will work well with others. Unfortunately, this is very much untrue. It is possible to have negative effects from an otherwise perfectly fantastic and powerful mantra because each person has different karmic blocks and tendencies which can lead to mantra allergy. In the best case, the mantra will simply not work but in the worst case, mental instability can occur. Also, a mantra that might be suitable at a certain time of one's life might not be suitable with the passage of time and the arising of hidden karmic patterns. Great caution is advised – ignorant seekers go where even angels fear to tread – picking up mantras like grocery from the supermarket is unwise.

To address the first obstacle and partially, the third as well, I recommend a progressive mantra yoga program for those who wish to pursue the mantric path:

1. Level 1 – Harmony: In this spiritual practice, the mantras

given are meant to transform the mixed-up and conflicted mind into a more harmonious and peaceful state. A set of mantras are given which are properly termed stotras which invoke the planetary, solar, and divine powers in reverence and proper sequence for different times of the day. This practice overcomes mental and emotional problems as well as removes obstacles in one's life path. These stotras have been declared safe and effective for all persons by generations of sages.

2. Level 2 – Unity: This is an advanced sadhana requiring a harmonious mind and strong concentration. It consists of a sandhya - that is a spiritual practice performed at certain transitional times of the day such as dawn or sunset. This sandhya is a universal one suitable for all men or women, regardless of religious affiliations as it invokes the power of Cosmic Consciousness, to transform the mind into unity consciousness or samadhi state.

3. Level 3 – Divinity: In this practice, the sincere seeker who has been able to transform his or her mind and achieve some level of samadhi consciousness is now initiated into his or her individual ishta mantra – the unique mantra that will lead to Self-realization. The teacher will need to perceive the correct mantra to give to the student.

Such a progressive program as outlined is consistent with the traditional and effective mantra yoga, reflecting the training that was in place in the past.

Level 1 Mantra Practice

Transforming the Mind

Spiritual Evolution

Each of us is a potential star!   More than that, each of us is potentially Divine, and can hold galaxies in the palm of our hands. Such are the teachings of the Ancients. We've been brought up to reject such wild concepts. Wealth and position in society are now the desired goals to strive towards. In our hearts we feel the hollowness of realizing such lofty aspirations, but nonetheless, follow the prescribed rut.

Reality as perceived by the sages is much more glorious. The earth itself is but star-dust, born from stellar debris, and is constantly evolving. From the earth we obtain our bodies, and from our star, the Sun, we receive our life, our soul.

There is an impetus in earth matter to evolve.   The physical aspects of evolution have now assumed the loftiness of science due to the efforts of Darwin and his followers. Few dispute the evolution from single cell toward multi-cell organisms, from invertebrate to vertebrate, from reptiles to mammals. Although the real story is much more complex for scientific comfort and man's role as yet clouded by yawning gaps, it is a helpful analogy to the immensity that is spiritual evolution. The ancient masters of yoga have always recognized and taught evolution. In fact, the goal of these ancient spiritual scientists was to accelerate the evolutionary process.

It is well-known in the field of human psychology that a "normal human" limited to body and superficial mental consciousness is actually strongly influenced by the vaster unknown depths of the sub-conscious and unconscious.

The yogic scope is larger and encompasses the field of higher consciounsess - the "individual" body/mental consciousness is only one mode of a vaster framework of evolution to soul consciousness, universal consciousness and finally to naked and empty Being, from which all beings arise. This can be illustrated through our subtle body model in that the chakras or energy centers are also related to the corresponding centers of consciousness, as shown by Figure 6, and the sound modalities fo mantras for the *chakras* will have a positive evolutionary effect on consciousness, as well.

When human evolution advances to the highest level, the subconscious mind is cleared, ego is dissolved and super-consciousness is awakened. Even more than ordinary human consciousness is light-years beyond animal consciousness, so super-consciousness is beyond the ordinary human intellect, logic and reasoning. Figure 7 shows the relationship of spiritual evolution and physical evolution.

When the highest level of evolution is not only isolated among a few exceptional individuals, but is prevalent in a society, then that society exists completely in harmony with Nature, beyond technology, religion and violence.

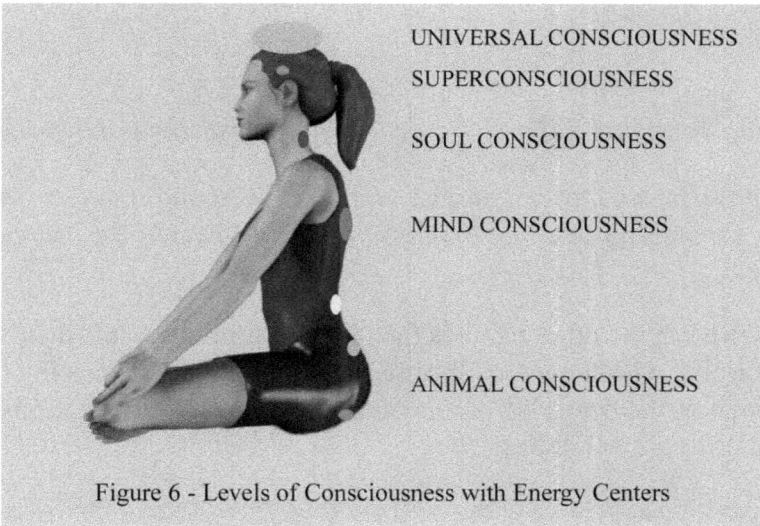

Figure 6 - Levels of Consciousness with Energy Centers

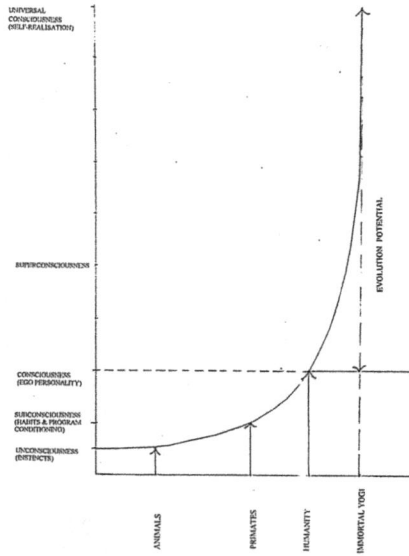

Figure 7
Spiritual Evolution and Physical Evolution

Two Ways of Life – the downward and upward paths

Pravritti means to live amidst worldly duties and interests with the senses and actions directed primarily towards the external world.

Nivritti, on the other hand, is the path of "turning back", the path of turning within towards spiritual contemplation, and placing the Divine at the center of our existence after fulfilling our familial and professional duties.

For as long as we live in Pravritti our thoughts turn mainly towards worldly things – to pleasure and hobbies and worrying about fame, position and possessions. Initially school and education occupy our thoughts, then later profession and family. Finally, in old age we worry about our health and our progeny.

Of course, based on tradition, it is proper and necessary for us to fulfill our responsibilities and duties to our family and society - there is a no problem with being comfortable or prosperous. However, if one cares about nothing else and is totally wrapped up in these temporary things, constantly grasping after them, believing that it is absolutely essential to "make or do" something, then their energies are wasted outwardly. When we strive after possessions and are never satisfied, then it is a sign that we are still on the downward path of pravritti.

What is the goal of life? The sages teach that it is an error to think that the goal in life is to experience and enjoy the world. What does enjoyment mean? A wise person knows that desires are never-ending. We are constantly hungry and thirsty, even if we have just eaten well. No worldly pleasures satisfy us forever. Desire soon rises anew. Only something long lasting and unchanging is able to give us true satisfaction. That which changes is unreal – only the eternal and unchanging Self is real.

If we follow one path we will inevitably reach where that path leads. When we turn our mind too much towards the outer world we lose contact with our inner world and to Divinity. Therefore the only way out of the illusion of Maya is through nivritti.

As we keep the mind free of worldly desires and turn towards the Divine, the attitude of nivritti should predominate, not just externally but more importantly inwardly. Neither money nor possessions make us inwardly rich - rather, true wealth lies in a peaceful heart and contentment. Only in nivritti can the soul permanently quench its thirst for happiness and knowledge.

One day, no matter how many life-cycles it takes, every human will attain perfection. The two ways of life are like two branches of a tree. The pravritti branch bends down towards the world, whereas the nivritti branch goes upwards towards divine consciousness. We will traverse both paths – when we tire of pravritti, then we will begin the nivritti cycle.

Restoring Light and Harmony

In yogic philosophy, all matter in the universe arises from the fundamental substrate called prakriti. From prakriti arises the three primary gunas or qualities that create the essential aspects of all nature—energy, matter and consciousness. These three gunas are tamas (darkness), rajas (activity), and sattva (lightness). All three gunas are always present in all beings and objects but vary in their relative amounts leading to various levels of material attachment and delusion.

Lord Krishna has said (BG 14:05 – 14:08):

The eternal embodied soul to the material body bound
The three-fold principle binding mind is found

Pure and good, illuminating sattva snare
Attachment to happiness and knowledge beware

Restless and passionate, intense selfish rajas craving
Attachment to desire borne on fruits of work saving

Ignorant and lazy, tamas delusion inducing wrap
Attachment to negligence and non-action soul trap

Understanding the gunas is critical to knowledge of human psychology. The mind is highly unstable and fluctuates under the changing dominance of the different gunas. The temporarily dominate guna acts like a lens that effects our perceptions and perspective of the world. When the mind is dominated by rajas it will experience world events as chaotic activity and it will react in a passionate and restless manner.

Yoga teaches that we have the ability to consciously alter the levels of the gunas in our bodies and minds. The gunas cannot be separated or removed in oneself, but can be consciously acted upon to encourage their increase or decrease. A guna can be increased or decreased through the interaction and influence of external objects, lifestyle practices and thoughts.

An important way to regulate these gunas in body and mind is through ayurvedic cooking which seeks to increase the sattvic, decrease rajasic and avoid the tamasic foods.

Sattvic foods are fresh, juicy, light, nourishing, sweet and tasty and give the necessary energy to the body without taxing it. It is the foundation of higher states of consciousness. Examples are juicy fruits, fresh vegetables that are easily digestible, fresh milk and butter, whole soaked or sprouted beans, grains and nuts, many herbs and spices in the right combinations with other foods.

Rajasic foods are bitter, sour, salty, pungent, hot and dry. They increase the speed and excitation of the nervous system and chaotic thoughts in the mind. It is the foundation of motion, activity and pain. Examples are sattvic foods that have been overcooked or oil-fried, foods and spices that are strongly exciting such as garlic and onions.

Tamasic foods are dry, old and decaying. They consume large amounts of energy while being digested. They are the foundation of ignorance, doubt, pessimism. Examples are foods that have been strongly processed, canned or frozen and/or are old, stale or incompatible with each other - meat, fish, eggs and liquor are especially tamasic.

Saints and seers can survive easily on sattvic foods alone but householders living in the world and have to keep pace with its changes also need rajasic energy. It is necessary to keep a balance as much as possible.

Since all gunas create attachment and thus bind one's self to the ego, it is necessary to transcend them. While the seeker should initially cultivate sattva, his/her ultimate goal is to transcend their misidentification of the self with the gunas and to be unattached to both the good and the bad, the positive and negative qualities of all life.

When one rises above the three gunas that originate in the body; one is freed from birth, old age, disease, and death; and attains enlightenment. (BG 14:20).

Level 1 mantras are all about developing sattva - refer figure 8

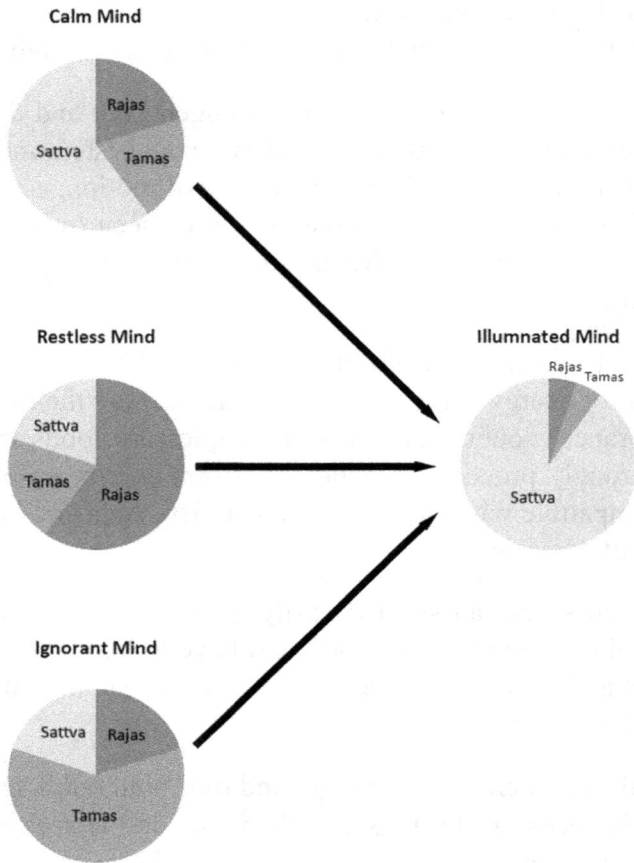

Calm Mind

Rajas

Sattva Tamas

Restless Mind

Sattva

Tamas

Rajas

Ignorant Mind

Sattva Rajas

Tamas

Illumnated Mind

Rajas Tamas

Sattva

FIRST LEVEL MANTRA
TRANSFORMATION OF THE MIND

Figure 8

Transformation of the Mind

Examples of Useful Mantras

Before we begin the first level mantra practice, it is useful to look at some of the related mantras that can be helpful in achieving an illuminated mind.

There are *mantras* which should be repeated aloud in order to have the desired effects on the external world, that is, the environment and physical body. There are also mantras which should be repeated mentally only, in order to internalize their effects for wholly spiritual purposes.

There are also some mantras which can be practiced both aloud and mentally. In general, we can repeat these powerful vibrations first, aloud, then in a whisper and finally mentally. These three modes of repetition give powerfully enhanced effects on the physical, energetic/ emotional, and mental/causal complex of human beings.

Mantra for Truth, Light and Immortality

The following is one *mantra* which has been repeated everyday by spiritual seekers for thousands of years and is one I recommend to chant before your daily practice:

Om
Asatoma Sadgamaya
Tamasoma Jyotirgamaya
Mrityorma Amritamgamaya.

O, Divine
Lead me away from untruth to Truth
Lead me away from darkness to Light
Lead me away from death to Immortality.

Repeat at three times aloud, three times in a whisper, and three times silently. The best time is before meditation in the morning.

Mantra for Commencement of Studies

It is traditional that before the commencement of studies and teaching, the following mantra is recited to establish the proper frame of mind and attitude towards the subject and prevent any misunderstanding between teacher and student:

Om
Saha naavavatu
Saha nau bhunaktu
Saha veeryam karavaavahai
Tejasvinaavaavadheetamastu
Maa vidvishaavahai.
Om
Shanti, shanti, shanti.

O Lord
Protect us (from misinterpretation)
Give us enjoyment (from our studies)
May we strive together (to arrive at the truth)
May our studies be thorough and free from error
May we be free from quarrel and full of mutual respect.
O Lord
Give us perfect peace.

A Mahavakya

The ancient seers expressed their profound insights into reality through certain mantric sayings called mahavakayas (literally, great sayings.) These mahavakyas are mantric because their vibrations can cause mental transformation and lead from normal consciousness to the higher consciousness that apprehended that level of reality. The difference between these mantras and most other types of mantras is that the practitioner is meant to reflect on the underlying meaning as well as experiencing the vibratory power of the saying. Most other types of mantras work through the vibratory power and resonance with higher consciousness and may have no meaning or even where meanings are attributed for easier remembrance, the meaning is to be discarded so as not to excite mental activity.

The following is the mahavakya from the Brihadaranyaka Upanishad:

Aham Brahm-Asmi
I am one with Cosmic Consciousness

This should be repeated aloud and silently as the mood strikes you. It should be repeated day and night. Reflect on the meaning continuously.

This one saying leads to apprehension of the great life questions – such as 'Who am I?" "What is death?" "Is there God?" "What is my relationship with God?" and many others that arise in the course of contemplation. The mind must be brought back to the mahavakya for it holds the key to the answers, which will appear like bolts of lightning in the receptive mind.

It is important to have some perspective when practicing this technique because one can enter into delusional mental states such that one will think that "I am God." Keep in mind that although a glass of water taken from the ocean has the properties of the ocean water, it is only a minute portion of the whole and is separated from the ocean by the glass holding it – the glass of water is not the ocean. Only when the glass of water is returned to the ocean does it become merged with the whole.

Harness Creativity At Will

Whether you are a creative in the traditional sense of being an artist, musician and writer, or need to apply creativity into solving your problems such as a programmer or marketer, we can learn to harness our powers of creativity better with yogic techniques.

One of the easiest ways is to change the active brain lobe at will using breathing techniques. The right brain is correlated with higher inspiration and creativity and the right brain is connected with activity of the left nostril. It has been well known for thousands of years that our nostrils are not always both opened fully at the same time – one nostril is usually more open than the other and this changes every few hours. It has been discovered that when the left nostril is more opened, there is more activity on the right brain. Therefore, if you find that your right nostril is more opened and you need to harness your creativity rather than your rational, analytical powers, you should change the dominant nostril to the left side – close your right nostril with the right index finger and breathe only through the left nostril for about 15 minutes. This forced left nostril breathing will activate the right brain activity.

Another method is to utilize the harmonic vibration from one of the creativity mantras of Saraswati, who is the cosmic creative power and can be accessed for our microcosmic activities. The following is a Saraswati stotra which is chanted aloud:

Ya kundendu tushaar haara dhavalaa,
ya shubra vastraavrutaa
Ya veenavara danda manditakaraa,
ya shweta padmaasana
Ya brahamaachyuta shankara prabhrutibhi:
Devyai sadaa vanditaa
Saamaan paatu Saraswati bhagawati,
ni:shesha jaadyaa pahaa.

O godess Saraswati, pure and radiant as the full moon and the frost, wearing a garland of jasmine flowers in the your white robes, seated on your lotus throne; with the veena on your lap; O one from whom has originated the three, Brahma, Vishnu and Shankara, O one, who is surrounded and respected by all gods, may you bless and protect me and remove every vestige of laziness and sloth from inside me.

This mantra should be chanted at least 27 times before undertaking any creative efforts. Those who undertake creative work at all times, usually chant this mantra 108 times every morning.

Guidelines for Practice

1. Regular practice - It is important to establish the habit of daily practice at a fixed time because the mind is more easily controlled and slowed down when it is conditioned to expect the practice.

2. Set aside a space for mantra practice – although it is best to have a room for your meditation, it is not necessary. However, a partitioned or screened off space within a room that only you will use can be very helpful. Your practice sets up a vibration that can help to induce a quiet mind – this can be disturbed by others accessing the space.

3. The most effective times for meditation are at dawn and dusk. Just before sunrise, the mind is clear and undisturbed by your daily activities. It is more easily rewired during these times. If it is not possible to practice early in the morning, choose a time when you are relatively undisturbed and mind can be calmed – choose a time that can become a regular routine.

4. The best directions to face are east to align with the movement of the earth or north to align with the magnetic field.

5. Sit in a comfortable and steady posture with head and neck erect but relaxed. This helps to steady the mind and promote concentration. Such a posture enables the energy currents to travel

unimpeded from the base of the spine to the top of the head. The legs should form a triangle, a firm base for long duration – any cross-legged posture will work. If it is not possible to sit on the floor, then sitting on the edge of a chair or even lying down on your back are acceptable alternatives.

6. Calm the mind and practice slow deep breathing for a few minutes before commencing the mantra repetition.

Guidance for mantra practice

1. Mind and Emotions

Preparation: take time to get into the right frame of mind. If you are tired, relax and drink a cup of tea first or do some light stretches to release tension.
Patience: Accept whatever occurs during your practice. Accept that changes take time and effort - there is no instantaneous or miraculous overnight transformation.
Will-power: Strengthen your will. Practice even when you don't feel like it - practice even if you are having doubts.
Harmony: Let the mantras harmonize with your body and mind. Feel their vibrations in and around you.
Concentration: Let go of disturbing thoughts and don't let the repetition of the mantras become mechanical - be absorbed in the mantras without losing awareness.

2. Obstacles:There will be blocks and barriers to your practice. With a combination of patiencce andwill-power, you can overcome all the obstacles. The major ones include:

Boredom: the lower mind is a monkey mind and is

always looking for new experiences and resists repetition. With heightended awareness, you will recognize this fidgety reaction to your practice.

Daydreaming: it is easy to slip into this semi-awake state and let the sub-conssious mind dictate your consciousness - it is especially attractive when our deepest fantasies and desires are played out. Once you become aware of the this state, resist it and take a few deep breaths to return to your practice.

Ego blocks: There can be many traps for the unwary. Due to our own pride, we may feel that we can alter the mantra or that it feels better in a different way. We may doubt the efficacy of the mantra or the giver of the mantra. On the other hand, we may feel over-confident of our accomplishments from the mantra, especially when certain powers or siddhis manifest - a great trap that must be resisted. Using the awareness or knowledge that comes from the mantra practice for material benefits or to show off can result in twisting the purpose of your practice and delay the ultimate result of Self-Realization.

3. **Cultivate ethical behavior** - throughout one's spiritual practice, one should keep in mind that the ultimate goal is realization of our true nature and that our behavior reflects our state of consciousness. Bad behavior increase karma and ignorance while positive behavior loosens karmic blocks. The lessening of karma removes obstacles to the practice and brings about a clarity and purification of mind.

Level 1 Mantras

The following are the mantras that should be cultivated and practiced to clarify the subtle bodies and the mind so that the practitioner becomes suitable to proceed to the higher levels of mantra practice. It will take some time to learn the mantras and once they are learned, each needs to be repeated a minimum of three times and maximum of nine times at the appropriate times of the day. Although, these mantras have been related to different times of the day, they can be practiced anytime that the aspirant feels the urge or need.

Early Morning Mantras

Karaagre vasate laxmi,
Kara moole saraswati
Kara madhye tu govinda,
Prabhate kara darshanam.

At dawn, let us look at our palms and praise mother Laxmi who resides at the tips of our fingers,
Let us praise mother Saraswati who is at the base of the palm,
and
Let us praise Lord Vishnu who resides in the middle of our palms.

Rudra Shivananda

Samudra vasane devi parvata stana mandate
Vishnupati namastubhyam Paadasparsham kshamasva me.

O, mother earth who is dressed by the oceans
Whose breasts are splendid as the mountains
O, auspicious one, please forgive me for I walk on you this day.

Vakratunda Mahakaaya
Surya koti sampaprabha: Nirvighnam kuru me deva,
Sarva karyeshu sarvadaa.

O, Lord Ganesha, of the large body and curved trunk,
Who shines like a million suns,
Please free my life and work from obstacles forever.

Adi deva namastubhyam
Praseeda mama bhaskara,
Divakara namastubhyam,
Prabhakara namostute.

O first among the gods, I salute you.
One who gives light,
One who causes the day, I salute you
One who makes the light, I salute you.

Brahma muraari tripuraantakaari
Bhanu shashi bhoomisuto Buddhascha
Guruscha shukra: shani rahu ketava
Kurvantu sarve mama suprabhaatam.

Let the gods brahma, vishnu, shiva,
The sun, the moon, mars, mercury, Jupiter, venus, Saturn, the
north and south moon's node,
Make my morning auspicious for me.

Before Going to Work or Before Meditation

Guru Brahma Guru Vishnu Gurudevo Maheshvaraa
Guru saakshaat parabrahma tasmay shree guruve namaha.

> I salute my spiritual preceptor who to me is
> the three aspects of divinity,
> Truly, the embodiment of the supreme reality.

> *Om asato maa sadgamaya,*
> *Tamaso maa jyotirgamaya*
> *Mrityoma amrutam gamaya*
> *Om shanti, shanti, shanty.*

> O lord, lead me from the unreal to the real,
> Lead me from darkness to light,
> Lead me from death to immortality.
> Peace, peace, peace.

Ya kundendu tushaar haara dhavala, ya shubhra vastraavrutaa,
Ya veenavara danda manditakaraa, ya shweta padmaasana,
Ya brahmaachyuta shankara prabhrutibhi:
Devyai sadaa vanditaa
Saamaan paatu Saraswati bhagawati, ni:shesha jaadya pahaa.

> O mother Saraswati, pure and radiant as the full moon and the
> frost,
> Wearing a garland of jasmine flowers in your white robes,
> Seated on your lotus throne with your veena on your lap,
> O, mother of the gods, who is surrounded and respected by all,
> May you bless and protect me and remove every trace of
> laziness from me.

After lunch or afternoon

Brahmaarpanam brahma havir brahmaagnau,
Brahmanaahutam, brahmaiva tena gantavyam,
Brahma karma samaadhinam.

The whole of creation is the projection from the divine,
The process of giving is the divine,
whatsoever is given is the divine
The giver is divine, the medium of giving is divine,
One who in his actions is totally absorbed in the divine,
attains to the divine.

Evening

Ya devi Sarvabhuteshu maatru repena sansthitaa
Namastasyayi namastasyayi namastasyayi
Namo namaha.
O supreme goddess who dwells in all living beings
as the kind loving mother,
Please accept my humble salutations over and over again.

Padmaasanesthite devi parabrahma swaroopini
Sarvadhukha hare devi
Mahalakshmi namostute.

O goddess who sits on the lotus,
the manifestation of supreme truth,
Remove all suffering from me,
O mother of the universe, I salute you.

Om sarva mangala maangalye shive sarvartha saadhike
Sharanye tryambake gauri
Narayani nomostute.

O goddess who bestows well-being and happiness to all,
I surrender to you, O spouse of Lord Shiva,
I offer my salutations.

Night time before bed

Om sarveshaam swastir bhavatu
Sarveshaam shantir bhavatu
Sarveshaam poornam bhavatu
Sarveshaam mangalam bhavatu.

May all beings become fortunate,
May all beings arrive at peace,
May all beings achieve perfection
May all beings be blessed.

Om sarve bhavantu sukhinaha sarve santu niraamayaaha
Sarve bhadrani pashyantu maa kasschit dukhkha bhaakbhavet

May all beings attain happiness, may all be healthy
May all enjoy good fortune and one suffer misery and sorrow.

Kara charana kritam vaak
Kaayajam karmajam vaa
Shravana nayaana jam va
Maanasam vaaparaadham
Vihitam avihitam vaa

[59]

Rudra Shivananda

Sarvam etat kshamasva
Jaya jaya karunaabdhe
Shri mahaadeva shambo.

Whatever wrongs I have done
Whether by my hands or feet, speech, body or action.
Arising from hearing, seeing or of the mind,
Committed or omitted – please forgive all.
You are the victorious ocean of compassion, O Lord.

Om Purnamada Poornamidam
Poornaat Poornamudachyate
Poornasya Poornamaadaaya
Poornamevaa Vashishyate
Om Shanti, Shanti, Shanti

That is perfect, this is perfect
What comes from such perfection
Is again truly perfect
What remains if perfection is negated
Is yet again perfect
May there be peace, peace, peace!

Level 2
Mantra Practice for Unity

By now, you may be have reaped the fruits of practicing the Level 1 mantras and be eager to proceed on to the practices of Level 2. Please do restrain yourself for a little longer. There is plenty of time to practice and sufficient practices to quench your thirst for powerful spiritual techniques. Before starting a journey, it is best to understand the roadmap, learn to recognize certain landmarks, avoid the dangers and be prepared for any detours and obstructions.

In a similar manner, the potential practitioner should have a basic understanding of the spiritual models underlying a specific spiritual system of Self-Realization.

For the system of MantraYoga, it is necessary to examine the following models before getting started. It is highly recommended that the practitioner return to study them over the course of time in order to gauge one's progress and to seek help for any wrong turns.

There are four models which have a direct and relevant bearing on all spiritual practice:

1. The progressive and iterative eightfold path of spiritual awakening annunciated by the yogic sage Patanjali.

2. The model of higher consciousness described by Patanjali in his Yoga Sutras - especially the samadhi states.

3. The material involution model from gross to subtle matter and to subtlest matter that describes the evolution of the spiritual dimension. This Tattva model is necessary to understand the impact and effect of the techniques.

4. A subtle anatomy model covering the 5 bodies and the chakra/nadi system for understanding the operation of the techniques. We have already covered the basics of this model in the previous section for Level 1. However, it is necessary to keep those concepts in mind when moving forward.

The Eightfold Path of Spiritual Awakening

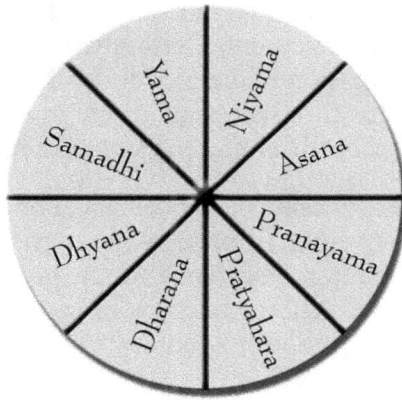

Patanjali's Ashtanga

Figure 9

The Ashtanga Pada

Patanjali was a great yogi and sage who may have lived around 200 BCE. He is the reputed author of the first systematic work on the path and science of yoga. It is called the Yoga Darshana but in the West, it is known as Patanjali's Yoga Sutras.

Patanjali delved deeply into the psychology and the process of the yogic path rather than on any specific set of techniques and so his work is applicable to any system of yoga whether it is Mantra Yoga or Kriya Yoga or Kundalini Yoga.

The sage anunciated an eightfold path that comprised objective and subjective elements. It encompassed ethical considerations and super-conscious psychology.

The eightfold path comprises Yama, Niyama, Asana, Pranayama, Pratyahara, Dharana, Dhyana and Samadhi.

To understand the eightold path of Patanjali, it is necessary to remove the misconception that it is a ladder-like structure with each step leading to the next and one must move from one to the next in upward movement. Certainly, there is a measure of this step-wise progression in the model but the overall scheme is more like the spokes of a wheel and there is a cyclic nature the 'steps'. As the wheel rolls along, the steps are repeated.

After the yoga practitioner or sadhak has completed the cycle from step one to step eight, he or she will return to step one and so on. After each revolution, the steps become progressively deeper and higher in nature. After a number of revolutions, the speed reached blurs the steps and it becomes a continuous movement into higher consciousness.

Ultimately, step one and eight are merged and there is no longer any distinction between them – they contain each other. This may seem a little mystical but it actually quite sensible when you consider the probable behavior of a Self-Realized being. Proper and ethical behavior requires effort and will-power from a normal person but is natural and effortless from one who is Self-Realized.

Another way to look at the model is from the objective to the subjective or from external to internal progressively. As we practice, we transcend the objective world and attain to pure subjectivity. Then we move back to the objective but in an enhanced mode. The goal is to achieve a merging of the objective-subjective and the external-internal polarities in unity that is yoga.

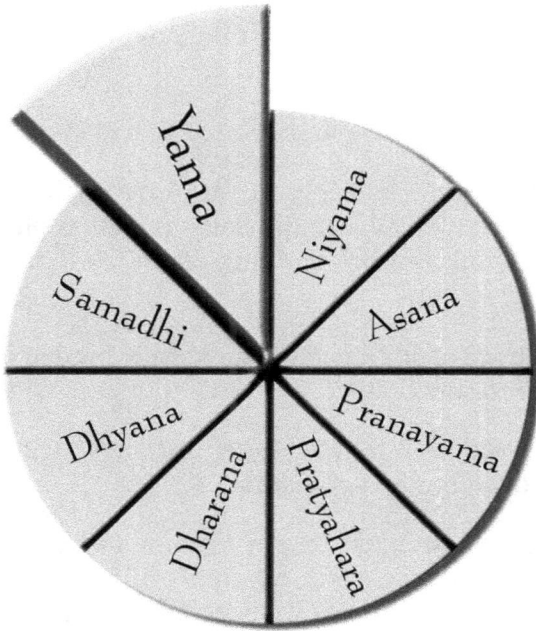

The first and most objective spoke of the wheel is Yama. This is popularly called the five restraints. They are:

- **Satya**: being truthful and refrain from lying

- **Ahimsa**: the refraining from harming other beings

- **Asteya**: refrain from stealing

- **Brahmacharya**: refrain from wasting one's energy on satisfying one's desires

- **Aparigraha**: refrain from being attached to the objective or subjective worlds

It is not my intention to go into depth about these five Yama, but to introduce them so that the practitioner has a basic concept. For more details, refer to my book – **The Yoga of Purification and Transformation.**

For our purposes here, we merely need to understand that:

1. these restrains apply to our everyday lifes. They need to be considered mentally, emotionally as well as physically, that is, we should refrain from harming others by thought, word or deed.

2. We are conditioned by our karmic burden in this life to break these restraints.

3. If we can follow these restraints, we are making progress in overcoming our Karma.

4. These restraints are only limiting factors from our ego-centric point-of-view. As we progress spiritually, they become natural and second-nature as we become more and more attuned to our True Self.

5. These restraints are the basic attributes of our True Self and from that perspective, require no effort and are no longer restraints.

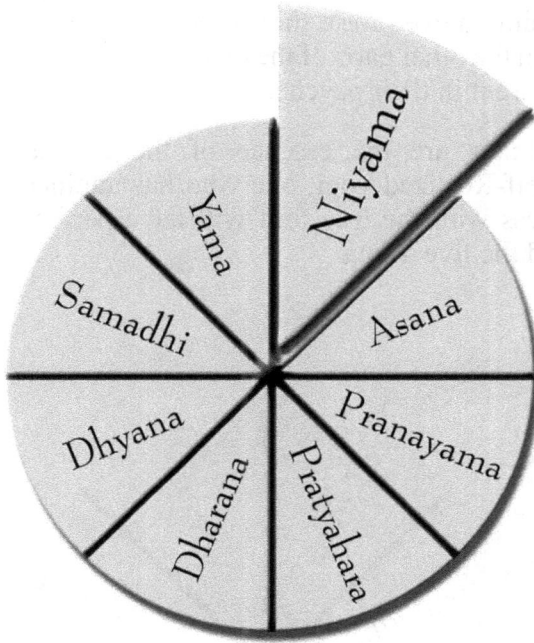

The second spoke in the wheel is that of **Niyama**. These are five positive attributes that we should develop. They are:

- **Saucha**: purity in our emotional, mental and intentional continuum.

- **Santosha**: contentment as an emotional and mental state.

- **Tapas**: control the five senses.

- **Svadyaya**: understanding and control of the mind.

- **Ishvar Pranidhana**: integrating one's will to the universal will.

These attributes are more refined and less observable than the five

Yama. They are transforming the emotional and mental attitudes of the spiritual practitioner. In the beginning, they require great effort to maintain even for s short time. However, as the student progresses in the other parts of the eight-fold path, these attributes become inherent in their psyche.

These attributes are the essence of the existential state of Being. A Self-Realized yogi, one who has attained to the unity consciousness with the true Self will have perfected these five Niyama and the five Yama.

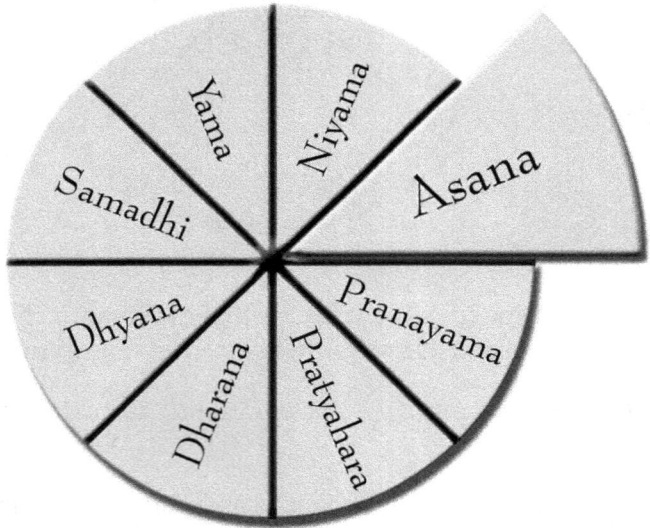

Asana (Physical Postures)

Asana is the practice of physical postures. It is the most commonly known aspect of yoga for those unfamiliar with the other seven spokes of Patanjali's *Yoga Sutra.* The practice of moving the body into postures has the obvious benefits for improved health, strength, balance and flexibility. On a deeper level the practice of asana, which means "a steady or abiding posture" in Sanskrit, is used as a tool to calm the mind and move into the inner essence of being.

The challenge of maintaining a pose offers the practitioner the opportunity to explore and control all aspects of their emotions, and concentration bringing about a unity between the physical body and mind. Asana is a way of exploring our mental attitudes and strengthening our will as we learn to release and move into the state of grace that comes from creating balance between our material world and spiritual experience.

As one practices asana it helps to quiet the mind, becoming both a preparation for concentration as well as a means of concentration in itself. The physical nature of the yoga postures becomes a vehicle to expand the consciousness that pervades our every aspect of our body.

The key to engendering this expansion of awareness and consciousness begins with the control of breath, the fourth limb called Pranayama. Patanjali tells us that the asana and the pranayama practices will bring about the desired state of health. The control of breath and bodily posture will harmonize the flow of energy in the organism, creating a fertile field for the evolution of the spirit.

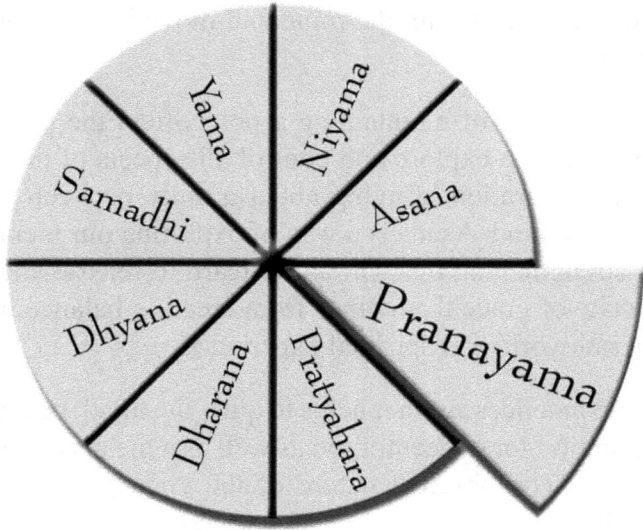

Pranayama (Breath Expansion & Control)

Pranayama is the expansion, control, and directing of the breath. Pranayama controls the life-force energy (prana) within the body, in order to restore and maintain health and to promote evolution. When the in-flowing breath is neutralized or joined with the out-flowing breath, then perfect relaxation and balance of body activities are realized. In yoga, we are concerned with balancing the flows of vital forces, then directing them inward to the chakra system and upward to the crown chakra.

Pranayama, or breathing technique, is very important in yoga. It goes hand in hand with the asana or pose. In the *Yoga Sutra*, the practices of pranayama and asana are considered to be the highest form of purification and self-discipline for the mind and the body, respectively. The practices produce the actual physical sensation of heat, called tapas, or the inner fire of purification.

It is taught that this heat is part of the process of purifying the nadis, or subtle nerve channels of the body. This allows a more healthful state to be experienced and allows the mind to become calmer. As the yogi follows the proper rhythmic patterns of slow deep breathing "the patterns strengthen the respiratory system, soothe the nervous system and reduce carnal craving. As desires and cravings diminish, the mind is set free and becomes a fit vehicle for concentration.

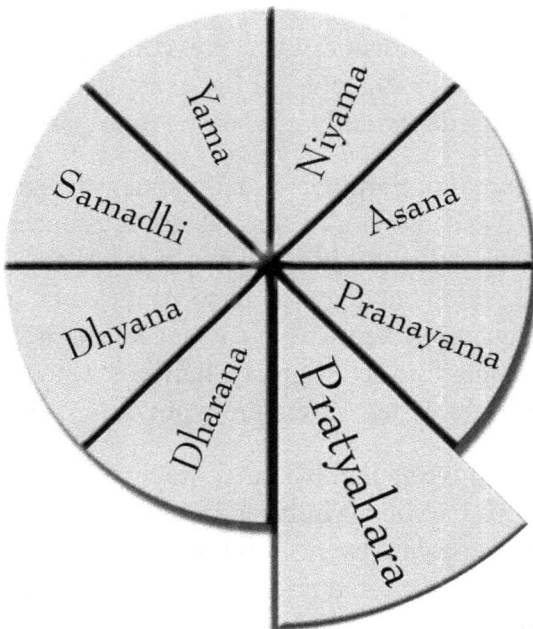

Pratyahara (Sense Withdrawal)

Pratyahara means drawing back or retreat. The word *ahara* means "nourishment"; pratyahara translates as "to withdraw oneself from that which nourishes the senses." In yoga, the term pratyahara implies withdrawal of the senses from attachment to external objects. It can then be seen as the practice of non-attachment to sensory distractions as we constantly turn to the path of self-realization and achievement of internal peace.

In pratyahara we sever this link between mind and senses, and the senses are no longer tied to external sources. When the vital forces are flowing back to the center within, one can concentrate without being distracted by externals or the temptation to cognize externals. It means our senses stop living off the things that stimulate and no longer depend on these stimulants and are no longer fed by them.

Pratyahara needs to occur when we concentrate because we should be absorbed in the object of concentration. As long as the mind is so focused internally, the senses follow it

No longer functioning in their usual manner, the senses become extraordinarily sharp. Under normal circumstances the senses become our masters rather than being our servants. The senses entice us to develop cravings for all sorts of things. In pratyahara the opposite occurs: when we have to eat we eat, but not because we have a craving for food. In pratyahara we try to put the senses in their proper place, but not cut them out of our actions entirely.

What causes emotional imbalance? Each of us is responsible for creating our emotional imbalance since we are continuously influenced by outside events and sensations. We can never achieve the inner peace and tranquility. This is because he or she will waste much mental and physical energy in trying to suppress unwanted sensations and to heighten pleasurable sensations. Such efforts tied to the avoidance or attraction to sensations can lead to emotional imbalances and psychosomatic illnesses.

Patanjali says that the above process is at the root of human unhappiness and uneasiness. When people seek out yoga to find that inner peace which is so difficult to capture, they find that it was theirs all along. In this sense, yoga is nothing more than a process which enables us to stop and look at the processes of our own minds in order to understand the nature of happiness and unhappiness, and then be able to transcend them both.

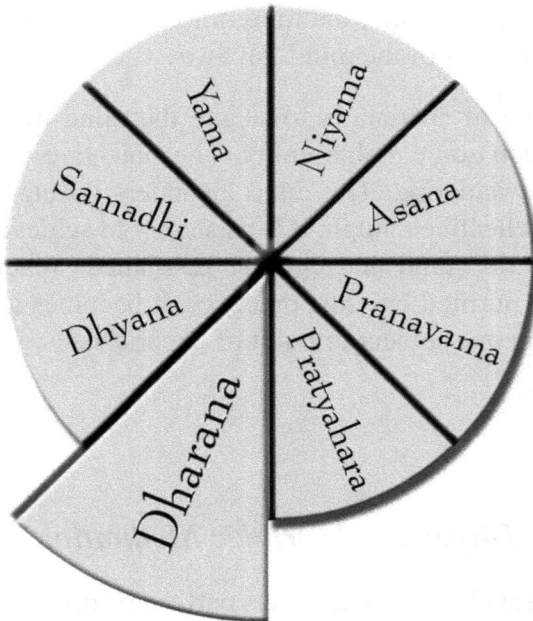

Dharana (Concentration)

Dharana means "immovable concentration of the mind". The essential idea is to hold the concentration or focus of attention on one object. "When the body has been tempered by asanas, when the mind has been refined by the fire of pranayama and when the senses have been brought under control by pratyahara, the sadhaka (seeker) reaches the sixth stage, dharana. Here he is concentrated wholly on a single point or on a task in which he is completely engrossed." The mind has to be stilled in order to achieve this state of complete absorption

In dharana we create the conditions for the mind to focus its attention on a single object or subject instead of going out in many different directions. Deep contemplation and reflection can create the right conditions, and the focus on this one point that we have chosen becomes more intense. We encourage one particular activity of the mind and, the more intense it becomes, the more the other activities of the mind fall away.

The objective in dharana is to steady the mind by focusing its attention upon some stable entity. The objective is to stop the mind from wandering. The mind meanders through memories, dreams, or reflective though. It is necessary to achieve the mental state where the mind and ego are restrained. When the mind has become purified by yoga practices, it becomes able to focus efficiently on one subject or point of experience.

Dhyana (Absorptive Meditation)

The seventh spoke is Dhyana - it is perfect absorption. It involves concentration upon an object or subject of focus with the intention of knowing the truth about it. The concept holds that when one is absorbed in an object the mind is transformed into the shape of the object. In this way, when one focuses on the divine, one becomes more reflective of that aspect of the divine – know and live that aspect.

During dhyana of the universal spirit, the consciousness is further unified by combining clear insights into distinctions between objects and between the subtle layers of perception. One learns to differentiate between the mind of the perceiver, the means of perception, and the objects perceived.

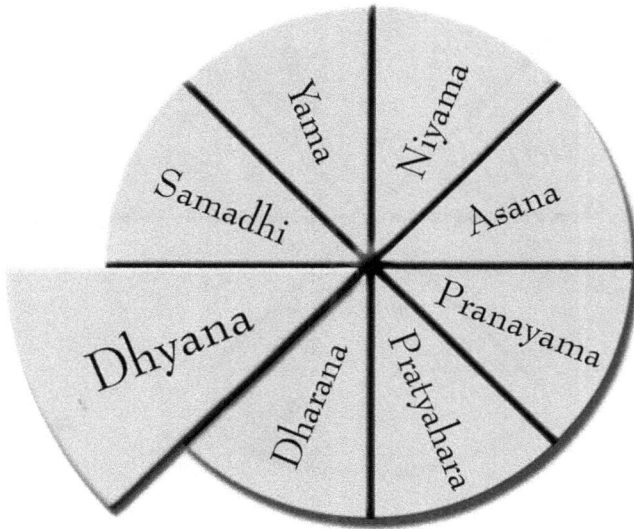

As we fine-tune our concentration and become more aware of the nature of reality we perceive that the world is unreal. "The only reality is the universal Self, or Divine, which is veiled by Maya (the illusory power). As the veils are lifted, the mind becomes clearer. Unhappiness and fear – even the fear of death – vanishes. This state of freedom, or Moksha, is the goal of Yoga. It can be reached by constant enquiry into the nature of things. Meditation becomes our tool to see things clearly and perceive reality beyond the illusions that cloud our mind.

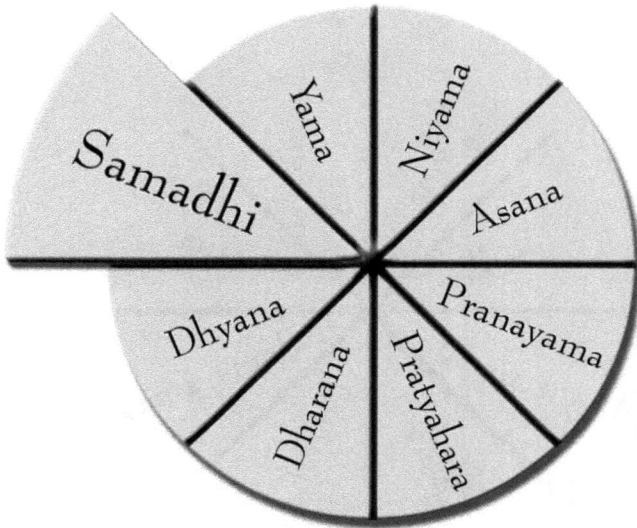

Samadhi (Unity Consciousness of Bliss)

The final spoke in the eight-fold path of Yoga is the attainment of Samadhi. Samadhi means "to bring together, to merge." There are a variety of samadhi states. In some states of samadhi the body and senses are at rest, as if asleep, while awareness is heightened in super-consciousness. In higher states of samadhi, called sahaj samadhi, it is possible to be in super-consciousness and still maintain the body and senses in operation.

During samadhi, we realize what it is to be an identity without differences, and how a liberated soul can enjoy pure awareness of this pure identity. The limited mind drops back into that unconscious pool from which it first emerged.

Samadhi is Yoga. There is an ending to the separation that is created by the "I" and "mine" of our illusory perceptions of reality. The mind does not distinguish between self and non-self, or between the object contemplated and the process of contemplation. The mind and the intellect have stopped and there is only the experience of consciousness, truth and Bliss.

The achievement of samadhi is a difficult task. For this reason the *Yoga Sutra* suggests the practice of asanas and pranayama as preparation for dharana, because these influence mental activities and create space in the crowded schedule of the mind. Once dharana has occurred, dhyana and samadhi can follow.

These eight spokes of yoga indicate a logical pathway that leads to the attainment of physical, ethical, emotional, and psycho-spiritual health. Yoga does not seek to change the individual; rather, it allows the natural state of total health and integration in each of us to become a reality.

Rudra Shivananda

The Tattva Manifestation Model

Before time, there was Shunyakasha – 'emptiness' or 'the void'. Shūnyākāsha is more than 'nothingness', it is an immense potency of dormant energy in which 'everything' exists in a latent state. Everything conceivable can be brought into existence, just like putting something on an empty sheet of paper.

As creation began, the divine, all-encompassing consciousness/energy in the composite Shiva/Shakti took the form of the first and original vibration manifesting as the sound 'Om'. This is the next composite of Nada/Bindu. Just like light, sound is vibration, and energy. Light and sound are the forms that the Divine Self takes in the Universe. OM is the reflection of the absolute reality.

It is said in the Vedas that Om is said in the Vedas, "Nada Rupa Parabrahma" – The form of the Supreme is vibration.

The vibration of Om symbolises the manifestation of the Divine in form. Om embraces all that exists - past, present and future, all spheres of the Cosmos, the world and its underlying reality, mind and matter, cause and effect, the path and the goal. The mantra Om is considered the 'name of the Creator' and used in conjunction with all other forms of the Divine. It therefores, comes most often at the beginning of all mantras to invoke the power of the Divine.

THE CYCLE OF
HUMAN MANIFESTATION

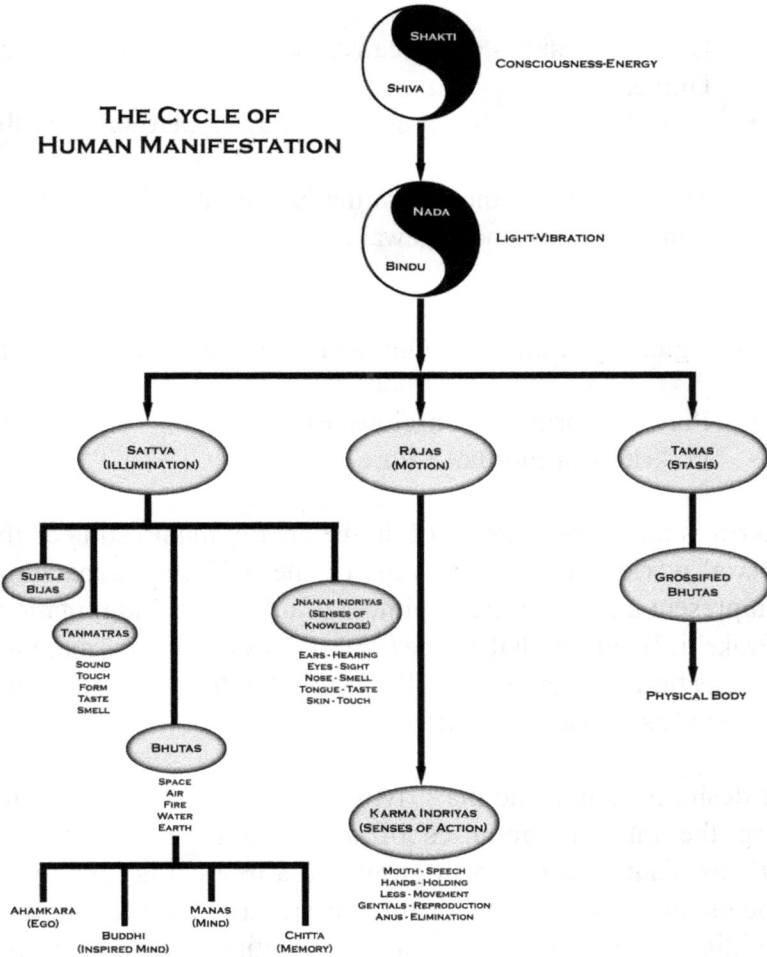

SHAKTI

SHIVA

CONSCIOUSNESS-ENERGY

NADA

BINDU

LIGHT-VIBRATION

SATTVA
(ILLUMINATION)

RAJAS
(MOTION)

TAMAS
(STASIS)

SUBTLE
BIJAS

GROSSIFIED
BHUTAS

TANMATRAS

JNANAM INDRIYAS
(SENSES OF
KNOWLEDGE)

SOUND
TOUCH
FORM
TASTE
SMELL

EARS - HEARING
EYES - SIGHT
NOSE - SMELL
TONGUE - TASTE
SKIN - TOUCH

PHYSICAL BODY

BHUTAS

SPACE
AIR
FIRE
WATER
EARTH

KARMA INDRIYAS
(SENSES OF ACTION)

MOUTH - SPEECH
HANDS - HOLDING
LEGS - MOVEMENT
GENTIALS - REPRODUCTION
ANUS - ELIMINATION

AHAMKARA
(EGO)

BUDDHI
(INSPIRED MIND)

MANAS
(MIND)

CHITTA
(MEMORY)

Figure 10
The Tattva Manifestation Model

When Om is realized in the form of the triad A-U-M the divine energy (Shakti) is united in its three elementary aspects as:

- Brahma Shakti - the creative power that manifests the Universe
- Vishnu Shakti - the preserving power that sustains the Cosmos
- Shiva Shakti - the liberating power that brings about transformation and renewal .

At the beginning of creation, Om manifested into the duality of:

- Purusha - original consciousness
- Prakriti - primordial nature

Prakriti is the eternal stream of divine energy manifesting as the material world and Purusha is the divine Self, the unchanging, omnipresent and omniscient witness of all events and mutations of Prakriti. To ensure that nature (Prakriti) would always maintain a connection to the divine (Purusha) the force of attraction developed as an aspect of Prakriti.

The desire for union and the striving for expansion are 'natural'; being the intrinsic impulses of nature. Why does the seed that was planted in the earth grow into a tree - it is due to the impetus for growth and duplication tht lies in its nature - uniting, unfolding, growing, multiplying, protecting, preserving and nourishing. In a higher level, the sages taught that 'loving' is the fundamental characteristic of Prakriti. Love contains the impulse for development and expansion, and this love is part of the Divine Being.

In a progressive sequence the three Gunas (essential qualities) and the five Bhutas (elementary principles) emanated from Prakriti. These form the basis of all manifestations, of all subtle and gross forms.

The three Gunas are:

- Rajas – activity, movement, restlessness, passion
- Tamas – rigidity, laziness, darkness, ignorance
- Sattva – harmony, light, purity, knowledge

The five Bhutas or universal elements are:

- Prithvi – Earth; solidity
- Apas – Water; fluidity
- Agni – Fire; transformation
- Vayu– Air; movement
- Akasha – Space; the matrix

Bhutas and Gunas are the primordial forces that have an effect on both the physical and astral planes. It is the Gunas that give the impetus to the elements to combine to form the material universe. Together, they influence all forms of life physically, psychically and spiritually from the beginning to the end of their earthly existence.

Through the multi-level combinations of these basic principles, the human body, with its highly complex organ, nerve and brain functions, comes into existence and the subtle bodies and mind are formed. The diverse interactions between the five gross Bhutas which form the physical body, are known as Prakritis (natural forces). There are twenty-five Prakritis that influence and regulate the systems of the body.

In order for the body to interact with the external environment, a series of sensory powers and activity powers were developed from the Sattva guna. These are the five jnana indriyas of hearing, sight, smell, taste and touch as well as the five karma indriyas of movement,holding, speech, reproduction and excretion.

The Cosmic forces are collected within the human body at certain central points, the chakras, which we have introduced in the first part for the Level 1 practices. These function like powerful power stations for the live force energy called prana.They draw in cosmic energy, transform, store and distribute it, and then radiate it out into the Cosmos again.

The Bhutas that combined to form the body as a dwelling for the soul will detach from one another at death and return to the Cosmos. The soul then continues to wander, waiting to produce a new form again under suitable conditions. This cycle is known as Chorasi Ka Chakra , 'The Wheel of Rebirth and Death'.

Unceasingly, the wheel of rebirth keeps turning, and the soul wanders through the circle of existence driven by their karmas(actions) . Human life offers a possibility of ending this cycle. The cyclic laws of nature also bind humans, but with the help of the intellect they are capable of exploring the world, themselves and also the superconscious states. On Earth, only humans are capable of realizing their True Self - that is why it is possible for us to emerge from the cycle of rebirth and, as a consequence, also help others to do so.

The practice of Yoga supports and accelerates the development of humans as it imparts to them knowledge of the true dimension of earthly life, its purpose and potential.

The evolution of consciousness attains fulfilment in the divine state of samadhi where knower, knowledge and the object of knowledge become one. Since the beginning of its existence the individual self has sought to gain knowledge about 'the Self'. While in Samādhi the self recognises that it and the one sought for are one and the same - therefore 'the Knower" and "the object of knowledge" are the same and so begins the blissful experience of unity, displacing the wrongly cherished illusion of duality.

This supreme knowledge is transmitted to us through two spiritual Tattvas, Anupada Tattva and Adi Tattva . Anupada Tattva (also called Guru Tattva) is the universal, divine principle that leads the creation from "darkness into light" – from unconscious existence to conscious existence. Patanjali called this principle Ishvar. Ādi Tattva is the divine Self - the Atma, expounded on within the Upanishads. Therefore it is also called Atma Tattva or Atma Gyana.

Self-Realised Yoga Masters are known also known as Tattva Darshi, the knowers of the Tattvas. Their knowledge and experiences are unlimited - transcending time, space and intellect. One who possesses self-knowledge and knowledge of the Tattvas has acquired the highest knowledge realisable by a human – with this one becomes the "knower of Divine" (Brahma Gyani) and the Self merges into the divine consciousness and becomes one with the Divine.

The Inner Psychic Functions

We must also understand the inner functions that guide the soul constantly - these four fucntions are necessary to investigate and guide our path of development - they are called the Antakharanas. They are also known as the "inner senses" - Antara Indiryas. They enable and guide our psychic and mental processes, and through them we can feel, think, understand and differentiate.

Rudra Shivananda

The Antahkaranas consist of:

- Manas - Lower or Sensory Mind
- Buddhi - Higher Mind or Intellect
- Chitta - Consciousness
- Ahamkara - Ego

Manas, the lower mind, is the realm of desires, feelings and thoughts. It is the connecting link between subconscious and conscious. It files away the impressions and perceptions from the external world in the 'storehouse of memories' and brings them out again based on karmic programs.

The mind does not judge or make a choice. It indiscriminately records all impressions just like a video camera or a tape recorder.

Buddhi (intellect) carries out the assessment and filtering of what reaches consciousness and what goes back down into the subconscious. On the basis of the impulse received from the intellect, the appropriate action is carried out by the mind.

The mind is constantly active in the waking state, and also when dreaming. We cannot stop the mind, but we are capable of guiding it. As we purify the mind by consciously thinking positively and repeating Mantra, and therefore ridding it of baser tendencies, the divine Self can then radiate through it.

Buddhi, the intellect , processes, co-ordinates and filters the sensory impressions. It decides which of them we accept and pursue further. Buddhi has two aspects, one egoistic and one selfless. The egoistic part is controlled by the ego and our weaknesses, whereas the selfless and non-personal principle is in harmony with the Divine guidance - this is known as viveka.

[84]

Viveka is like the 'butter'which is extracted from the 'cream' of buddhi. Through viveka we are able to differentiate between truth and untruth, right and wrong, good and bad. Viveka leads us to the knowledge that the material reality is relative, and guides our endeavours towards the Absolute, the Eternal.

Our ego-centric intellect develops in two different ways. Firstly, through everything we have learnt from childhood up to the present time. This logical knowledge helps us to cope with the tasks of daily life. And, secondly, it is formed through analysis, reflection, concentration (dharana) and meditation (dhyana). Wisdom and discrimination (viveka) ultimately develop from these. and leads to divine-centric buddhi.

Although our minds creates our mental condition, they are conditioned by our past and present life karmic programs. That is the reason we meet with life situations that we cannot master. Then we lose control of our thoughts and emotions, as for example in a fit of rage. How often have we said or done something when we were unable to control our emotions which we greatly regretted later on! That is why the cultivation of viveka is so tremendously important, not only for our worldly existence but also for our spiritual life.

Chitta, consciousness, forms the basis of our perceptions and knowledge. Like Buddhi it is shaped by the experiences of life; previous experiences, upbringing, culture and education mould the way in which we perceive, judge and value. Chitta determines the basic tendencies and colouring of our psyche.

Ahamkara, the ego, literally means "I am the doer". All our feelings, perceptions, ideas and desires are inextricably linked to ahamkara. The ego is that psychic authority that creates the illusion that we are autonomous to all the other independently

 Rudra Shivananda

existing individuals. From that we naturally derive the idea that the external world that confronts us is also an independent, separate reality.

However, Vedanta philosophy, which is also a philosophy used by Yoga, teaches us to see the unity- Divine - behind the variety of appearances. Only when we accept this reality, not just rationally but realise it within our consciousness, are we able to overcome the barrier of the ego and find unity in the Self.

The following mantra, in which we place all our actions into hands of the Divine, helps us to attain this way of thinking. It helps to attain to self-surrender or ishvar-pranidhan:

Naham Karta Prabhu Deep Karta
Mahaprabhu Deep Karta Hi Kevelam

I am not the doer.
It is Divine working through me.
The Divine alone is the doer.

Level 2 Mantra Yoga Sadhana

In the 2nd level of mantra practice, we will generally focus on one main mantram. However, there will be additional steps to learn and supplementary mantras and mudras that are required to unlock the power of the main mantram.

Two sadhanas that can be practiced by everyone is given. First is the Universal Sandhya dedicated to the universe and invoking the Brahma Gayatri mantra. In this practice, I've included explanation that would be helpful even if you choose not to make this your sadhana. Second is the Hamsa Sadhana invoking the divine Self - this one is shorter and less complicated. You can choose either one to do - both are effective.

As a reminder, please keep in mind:

1. Mantra practice overcomes old samskaras and prevents new karmic imprints from forming
    *   Prevent klista vrittis (afflicted thoughts) from arising
    *   Develop and maintain a single positive vritti

The single vritti or positive thought leads to purifying the mind, accessing the self-less buddhi. It will provide blessings in the form of siddhis or spiritual powers and eventually lead to liberaton of the cycle of rebirth (moksha).

2. It is possible to practice the Level 2 sadhanas without mantra diksha or initiation but if possible, such initiation can be helpful. Please note that Level 3 cannot be practiced without initiation.

3. In order to understand the sadhaana, keep in mind the different parts of a mantra introduced in Level 1:

Mantra = rishi + raja + devata + bija + shakti + kilaka

- Rishi: flow of grace, knowledge, power from the divine, a guide; seer of the mantram
- Raga: audible plus subtle sound
- Devata: presiding deity, informing power, aspect of god, personal relationship with an aspect of god that gives wisdom and virtue
- Bija: seed sound
- Shakti: dynamic energy released
- Kilaka: pillar, the driving force, will power, the key that unlocks the mantram for the power to be released; The unlocking of a mantra for power or protection
- Kavach: protection or armor
- Argala: bolt to open a closed door
- Kilaka: king-pin – pivot to furnish the key to open the hidden secrets
- Utkilane: to remove kilaka and argala

The kavach is an integration of parts utilizing the argala that rests on the kilaka

Universal Sandhya

This practice can be performed by all men and women regardless of age or ethnicity and invokes the power of the Divine within humanity. The word sandhya is derived from "sam" meaning perfect and "dhya" meaning meditation and so can be translated as the perfect meditation. A characteristic of all sandhyas (there are a number of different ones given in the sacred texts) is the principal of meditating on the characteristics of divine attributes as well as of the universal creation – the cosmos and on humanity – it joins the macrocosmic with the microcosmic.

The best times of practice for the sandhya can be ascertained from the derivation of the word "sandhi" meaning union and is the time between light and dark, that is, at dawn and dusk, the twilight times.

The Universal Sandhya is from the tradition of kula-dharma or the practice of universal love. This tradition considers humanity to be one family with its diverse members contributing to the whole according to their duties and obligations. The common bond is love and service to each other according to their capabilities and circumstances. This Universal Sandhya is derived from that given in the Mahanirvana Tantra.

Each Sandhya is founded on a core mantra. That of the Universal Sandhya is as follows:

Om Sach-chid-ekam Brahma

The Divine is the One, Self-Existent Universal Consciousness

This sandhya incorporates twelve different parts:

1. Nyasa: this is the placing of the mantric syllables on different parts of the body and serves to purify and consecrate the body as the temple of the Divine

2. Pranayama: the use of breath which is the vehicle of the life-force energy called prana to unite with the mantra

3. Dhyana – this is the meditation on the Divine attributes

4. Manasa Puja – a mental offering of the five elements to the Divine

5. Japa – the recitation of the core mantra for 108 times

6. External Puja – consecration of the actual objects such as flowers, ornaments or food

7. Praise of the Divine

8. Kavacha – the invocation of protection for the body and mind

9. Pranama or salutation to the Divine

10. Distribution or partaking of Prasad (consecrated food or drink)

11. Recitation of the Brahma Gayatri

12. Ending Pranama

I.   Rishi Nyasa

Each mantra has its seer or originator and for this sacred mantra, it is the divine aspect called Sadashiva. The meter with which it should be recited is called anushtup and its presiding deity is Brahma. This mantra encompasses all aspects of the aspirant's life – the fourfold goals of humanity – righteous living, enjoyment of the senses, accumulation of wealth and possessions, and liberation from suffering.

Shirasi Sadashivaya Rishaye Namaha
Salutations to the Rishi Sadashiva in the head

Mukhe Anushtup Chhandase Namaha
Saluations to the meter anushtup in the mouth

*Hridi Sarva-Antaryami-Nirguna-Parama-Brahmane
Devatayai Namaha*
Salutations to the supreme deity without attributes who
is in the heart

II.   Kara Nyasa – purification of the five fingers

Om Angusthabhyam Namaha
Salutations to Om on my thumbs

Sat Tarjanibhyam Svaha
My index fingers are offered to Sat

Chit Madhyamabhyam Vashat
Welcome to Chit on my middle fingers

Ekam Anamikabhyam Hum
Welcome to Ekam on my ring fingers

Brahma Kanishthabhyam Vaushat
Welcome to Brahma on my little fingers

III.   Anga Nyasa – purification of heart, head, crown of
         head, shoulders, eyes, and palms

Om Hridaya Namaha
Salutations to Om at the heart

Sach Chhriase Svaha
My head is offered to Sach

Chid Chhikhayai Vashat
Welcome to Chid on the crown of my head

Ekam kavachaya Hum
Welcome to Ekam on my shoulders

Brahma Netra-trayaya Vaushat
Welcome to Brahma in my three eyes

Om Sach-Chid Ekam Brahma Karatala-prishthabhyam Phat
Welcome to the palms of my hands

IV.   Pranayama

        Close the left nostril with your ring and middle fingers of
        the right hand. Then inhale gently through the right nostril
        while mentally reciting the main mantra (Om Sach Chid
        Ekam Brahma) four times. Then close the right nostril
        as well with the thumb and retain the breath with both
        nostrils closed while mentally repeating the main mantra
        sixteen times. Finally, remove the thumb and exhale
        through the right nostril while mentally repeating the
        mantra eight times. This is one round.

In the second round, the right nostril is closed with the thumb and the inhalation is through the left nostril for four mantra repetitions. The breath is held with both nostrils closed for sixteen repetitions, followed by exhalation through the left nostril for eight repetitions. The third and final round is a repeat of the first round.

V.   Dhyana - Meditate on a steady flame of life burning in the heart while reciting:

Hridaya-Kamala-madhye nirveshesham niriham
Hari-Hara-Vidhi-vedyam yogibhir dhyana-gamyam
Janana-marana-bhiti-brahmshi sach-chit-svarupam
Sakala-bhuvana-bijam Brahma chaitanyam ide.

I meditate on the Divine, the All-knowing,
within the lotus of my heart.
He is fre from all limiting attributes and desires and i
s the object of knowledge
To the highest intelligences like Brahma, Vishnu and Mahesh,
Who is known by mystic meditation by the contemplative sages
Who destroys the fear of birth and death
Whose essential nature is pure existence and knowledge and
Who is the cause of the entire universe

VI.   Manasa Puja

The mental offering of the five elements of material creation – solid, liquid, fire, gaseous and etheric – visualized as scents, flowers, incense, light and food while reciting the following mantras and with the two ring fingers, two thumbs, two index fingers, two middle fingers and finally the two ring fingers:

Lam prithvy-atmakam gandham
samarpayami namaha

I offer scent in the shape of solid matter
or the earth element

Ham akashatmakam pushpam samarpayami namaha
I offer flower in the shape etheric matter or the space element

Yam vayu-atmakam dhupam samarpayami namaha
I offer incense in the shape of gaseous matter or air element

Ram teja-atmakam dipam samarpayami namaha
I offer light in the shape of luminous matter or fire element

Vam amrita-atmakam naivedyam samarpayami namaha
I offer food in the shape of nectar or the water element

Join both hands with palms together in anjali mudra and recite
the following mantra:

Aim sarva-atmakam tambulam samarpayami namaha
I offer betel in the shape of the whole world

VII.   Japa

Recite the primary mantra 108 times:

Om Sach-Chit Ekam Brahma

Finish with the following:

Om Brahmarpanam astu
Let the fruit of all this go to the Divine

VIII.   External Puja

Offer and consecrate a food item such as doughnuts or cookies using the following mantra:

Brahmarpanam Brahma-havir
Brahm-agnau Brahmana hutam
Brahmaiva tena gantavyam
Brahma karma-samadhina

The Divine is the sacrificial vessel,
The Divine is the offering, ,
the Divine is the sacrificial fire
in which the offering is poured,
The offering is performed by the Divine to the Divine.

Close your eyes and recite 108 times
Om Sach-Chit Ekam Brahma

finishing with
Om Brahmarpanam astu

Open your eyes and recite 'Om Sach-Chit Ekam Brahma' 3
times aloud

IX.   Brahma Stotra

Recite the following praise to the Divine:

Om Namaste ste sarva-lok-ashrayaya
Namaste Chite vishva-rup-atmakaya
Namo-dvaita-tattvaya mukti-pradyya
Namo brahmane vyaapine nirgunaya

Salutations to the All-being, the refuge of all worlds
Salutations to the All-Intelligence

who is the soul of all forms of consciousness
Salutations to the One without a second,
O giver of salvation
Salutations to the All-pervading and without attributes.

Tvam ekam sharanyam tvam ekam verenyam
Tvam ekam jagat-karanam vishva rupam
Tvam ekam jagat-katri-patri-pahartri
Tvam ekam param nishchalam nirvikalpam

You are the sole refuge, You are the sole adorable
You are the One cause of the universe under all forms
You are the only creator, the preserver and
the Destroyer of the world
You alone are the highest immutable and ineffable.

Bhayanam bhyam bhishanam bhishananam
Gatih praninam pavanam pavananam
Mahochchaih padanam niyatri tvam ekam
Paresham param rakshakam rakshakanam

Dread of the dread, terror of the terrible
Refuge of all beings, purifier of all purifications
You alone rule the high-placed ones
Supreme over the supreme protector of the protectors.

Paresha prabho sarva-rup-aprakashin
Anirdaya sarvendriy-agamya satya
Achintyakshara vyapakavyaktatattva
Jagad-bhashakadhisha payad apatah

O supreme Lord in whom all things are, yet unmanifest in all
Imperceptible by the senses, yet the very truth
Incomprehensible, imperishable, all-pervading hidden essence

Lord and Light of the universe! Save us from harm.

Tad ekam smaramas tad ekam japaamh
Tad ekam jagat-sakshi-rupam namaamah
Sad ekam nidhaanam niralambamisham
Bhaavambhodhi-potam sharanyam vrajaamah

On that One alone we meditate,
the One alone we in mind worship
To that one alone the witness of the universe we bow
Refuge we seek with the One who is our sole Eternal support
The self-existent Lord, the vessel of safety
in the ocean of being.

X.   Brahma Kavacha
       The following verses serve to protect the body and give
       health:

Paramaatma shirah paatu,
hridayam parameshvaraha
Kanthkan paatu jagat-paatu
vadanam sarva drig bibhuh
Karau me paatu vishvaatmaa
padau rakshatu chin-mayah
Sarvaangam sarvadaa paatu
parama Brahma sanaatanam

May the supreme Spirit protect the head
May the supreme Lord protect the heart
May the protector of the world protect the throat
May the all-pervading, all-seeing Lord protect the face
May the Spirit of the universe protect my hands
May the essence of Intelligence protect the feet
May the eternal and supreme Spirit of the universe
protect the feet

May the eternal and supreme Spirit of the universe always
protect my body in all its parts

XI.   Pranama

Salutations to the supreme Spirit of the Universe:

Om Namaste Paramam-brahma
Namaste paramaatmane
Nirgunaya namas tubhyam
sad-rupaaya namo-namah

I bow to the supreme Spirit of the universe
I bow to the supreme Soul
I bow to Him who is above all qualities
I bow to the ever-existent again and again.

XII.   Distribution of food

The food that was blessed previously can be eaten by you
and / or given to others to eat. It is meritorious to offer
such food to others – bring it to the office and distribute
to your co-workers, or give to your children to bring to
school for sharing with their classmates.

XIII.   Brahma Gayatri

This mantra is recited 108 times:

Parameshvaraaya vidmahe
Paratattvaaya dhimahi
Tanno Brahma prachodayat

May we know the supreme Lord
Let us contemplate the supreme essence and
May that Spirit direct us.

XIV.   Final Pranama

Recite the pranama mantra as in XI.

> *Om Namaste Paramam-brahma*
> *Namaste paramaatmane*
> *Nirgunaya namas tubhyam*
> *sad-rupaaya namo-namah*

I bow to the supreme Spirit of the universe
I bow to the supreme Soul
I bow to Him who is above all qualities
I bow to the ever-existent again and again.

Rudra Shivananda

Hamsa Mantra Sadhana

The mantra of the True Self or spirit is Hamsa, sometimes also known as "Sa Aham" or "So Hum". It also means the swan and is the symbol of the freed soul. It is said that our breath constantly chants the Hamsa with the incoming breath sounding the "Sa" and the outgoing breath sounding the "ham" – in a mystical manner, the incoming breath is offered to the outgoing in a constant cycle that is called the ajapa-japa mantra.

In this mantra practice, there is a deepening and connecting of the body and mind with the consciousness, through touching, at the tips of the fingers by the action of the thumb as well as to various other parts of the body. This mantra-mudra practice is a great help in keeping awareness of the divine energy of the mantra throughout the day while immersed in our activities.

Opening Prayer

Om
Guru Brahma, Guru Vishnu
Guru Devo Maheshwaraha
Guru Sakshat Param Brahma,
Tasmai Shri Gruve Namaha

Shri Guru Paramatma Devata
Ham Bijam Sa Shaktihi Krom Kilakam
Shri Guru Prasada Siddyarthe Jape Viniyogaha

Kara Nyasa: Charging the fingers

Thumb: Point the thumbs upwards on both hands while chanting
Om Ham Sam Surya Atmane
Angushta-bhyam Namaha

I meditate on God within the solar circle - Salutations.

Index Finger: Roll the thumb over your index finger on both hands, while chanting -

Om Ham Sim Sarna Atmane
Tarjane-bhyam Namaha

I meditate on God in the Moon - Salutations.

Middle Finger: Roll the thumb on the middle finger of both hands, while chanting -

Om Ham Sum Niranaja Atmane
Madhyama-bhyam Namaha

I meditate on God on the middle finger as
attributeless pure consciousness - Salutation

Ring Finger: Roll your thumb on the ring fingers, of both hands while chanting -

Om Ham Saim Nira Bhasa Atmane
Anami-Kabhyam Namaha

I meditate on the invisible Atman on the
tip of the ring finger - Salutations.

Little Finger: Roll your thumb over the little finger of both hands, while chanting -

*Om Ham Saum Atanu Sukshma Atmane
Kanishtika-bhyam Namaha*

I meditate on the subtlest Atman on the
tip of the little finger - Salutations.

Palms: Join the palms and chant the following -

Prachodayat Sarvat-manei, Karatala

Backs of Hands: Touch the backs of the hands alternately with the palms and chant -

*Om Ham Saha Avyakta Atmane
Kara Tala Kara Prashta-bhyam Namaha*

I meditate on the unmanifest Atman on my palms - Salutations.

AngaNyasa : charging the body

With the fingers of the right hand, touch the heart center and chant:

*Om Hum Sam Surya Atmane
Hrida-yaya Namaha*

Light of light, the spirit of the solar deity,
I meditate on you in my heart.

With the fingers of the right hand, touch the forehead and chant:

*Om Hum Sim Sim Atmane
Shirase Swaha*

Abode of peace, the spirit of the moon,
I meditate on you in my forehead.

With the fingers of the right hand, touch the top of the head and chant:

Om Hum Sum Niranjana Atmane
Shikhayei Vaushat(u)

Pure Consciousness; nameless, formless truth,
I meditate on you at the crown of my head.

With the fingers of the right hand, touch the shoulders with the arms crossing in front and chant:

Om Hum Saim Nirabhasa Atmane
Kavachaya Hum

Invisible Universal Spirit, be my armor of protection.
I meditate on you in the upper part of my body.

Touch the right eye and chant,

Om Hum Saum

Touch the left eye and chant:

Atanu Netra

I invoke the energy which pierces the veil of ignorance
into my three eyes

Touch the third eye and chant:

Tra-yaya Vaushat(u)

[103]

Rudra Shivananda

Place your hands above the head, palms together. On the word "Phat" clap four times. This opens the energy channels above the head leading to the higher self:

Om Ham Saba Avyakta Atmane

HiddenTruth in this entire creation,
in your Holy Name I command
all demons and negativity to leave me and be destroyed.

Astraya Phat

May this vibration destroy the demons and negativity.

Main Discipline:

Chant the mantra below 108 times or more:

Om Hamsa Hamsaya Vidmahe
Paramahamsaha Dhimahi
Tanno Hamsa Prachodayat

Level 3
Mantra Practice for
Self-Realization

Higher Consciousness

In his Yoga Sutras Patanjali describes three processes that will lead us to the supreme state of consciousness – dharana, dhyana and samadhi.

- Dharana means concentration. In concentration we direct our consciousness towards a single object (for example, a Bīja Mantra), withdrawing it completely from all other things. For this it is crucial that we focus our attention totally on a single point.

- Dhyana is meditation. This is the next step after concentration when the "I" begins to dissolve in the object. This is the preliminary stage to samādhi. One cannot "learn" meditation. When body and mind are correctly attuned and have become quiet and pure the meditative state occurs by itself – just as sleep overcomes us by itself when we go to bed in the evening.

- Samadhi is the unity consciousness in which knower, knowledge and object of knowledge unite. I would like to know. I am the knower. I would like the knowledge. With the union of these three points of view the certainty and experience of "I am that – SO HAM" occurs.

Unity Consciousness cannot be experienced by the intellect alone - only when knowledge, knower and object become one. In the realization of the unity of SO HAM (I am that) all questions are answered and all desires fulfilled - the knower no longer exists, knowledge is no longer desired and there is no knowledge to acquire or any object to know. In the fullness of perfect existence all desires are extinguished.

To have this experience means realization of the truth – Self-Realization and God-Realization. Shankarāchārya praised the God-Realized, liberated consciousness in the following stotra:

> I am not this mind, nor intellect, ego or consciousness,
> Nor the Gyāna Indriyas or the Tattvas.
> My form is pure consciousness and absolute bliss
> I am chidananda rupa, Shiva, the Supreme Self.
>
> I am neither the five Prānas nor the seven Dhātus,
> Nor the five Koshas, nor this bundle of Karmas
> I am chidananda rupa, Shiva, the Supreme Self.

In me exists neither attachment nor duality,
Neither greed nor jealousy, neither hate nor anger.
I have nothing to do with the illusion of the ego,
And also I am not bound by the four laws of the Purushartha
I am chidananda rupa, Shiva, the Supreme Self.

I have neither sin nor virtue, nothing to do with either happiness
or sorrow,
Or with Mantras, pilgrimages, the Vedas or ceremonies
I am neither the food, nor the one nourished, nor the enjoyer
I am chidananda rupa, Shiva, the Supreme Self.

I am the Ātmā, immortal and unborn
Time, space and death have no power over me
I have neither father nor mother, neither relatives nor friends
No Guru and no student
I am chidananda rupa, Shiva, the Supreme Self.

I am desire-less and formless.
I exist in all living beings
I am not bound, nor require liberation
My form is truth, consciousness and bliss
I am chidananda rupa, Shiva, the Supreme Self.

What is the nature of the consciousness of one whose Self is established in reality and truth? How do they see others? How do they see their surroundings? What thoughts and emotions exist in the consciousness of such a realized one? How do they live in the world?

Realized souls can only be recognized with the eyes of the soul. Outwardly they appear exactly the same as anyone else. They eat, sleep, speak, laugh and go about their daily duties the same as others. But with deeper reflection the differences are noticeable.

A peaceful nature, all-understanding goodness, purity, splendor and a quiet dignity radiate from a God-Realized soul.

The unity consciousness of Samadhi and the liberation of Self-Realization occur in the thousand-petalled lotus (Sahasrara or crown chakra). It opens when we follow one of the Yoga paths with perseverance and devotion – the path of Raja Yoga or Kriya Yoga with discipline and practice, the path of Karma Yoga with selfless service, the path of Bhakti Yoga with devotion to God, or the path of Gyāna Yoga with study and renunciation. It is also said that we need Guru Kripa or the grace of the divine teacher.

The Masters have always counseled that: "One should not change one's inner vision". This means that we should remain faithful to the chosen path, Master or Ishta-devata (aspect of divinity) and not constantly change our beliefs or objectives. To reach the top of a mountain we should stay focused on the goal and move forward – do not to turn back or go around in circles.

Beware of the ego – never think that you are so great that you do not need guidance or discipline. It is a trap that some fall in – to think of oneself as the divine spirit, when one has not yet realized that truth – it is pure theory and does not align with reality.

Many things in life nourish the ego and cause a person to feel pride - youth, beauty, money, education, ethnic origin and social status. These are superficial factors caused by our previous good karma. We should make good use of these positive factors to help ourselves and others so that we can decrease our future bad karma. Instead, the ego influences us to abuse our good karma and produce bad karma for our future.

It is good to remember we have no control over even our own body - today strong and healthy, tomorrow perhaps weak and ill. It is best to surrender yourself to the Divine and devote ourselves to righteousness. We must clear our karmas and purify the ego so that he self or jiva can detach itself from the five koshas that veil it and hamper its free development. In this phase of development we are occasionally in an extremely vulnerable and disagreeable state – comparable to a snake when it sheds its skin. During the period that the snake is shedding its skin it can see nothing, is almost unable to move and also cannot eat. However, once it is fully released from the old sheath it is free and in full possession of its power. And so, when the jiva soul has rid itself of all fetters and reaches the Sahasrara Chakra, in that same moment it perceives the full light of truth.

It is difficult to determine what came first – the seed or the tree, the fruits or the karma. For eternity, the seed has grown from the plant, and the plant from the seed, in an inexhaustible sequence. In the same way an action produces a karmic reaction, and this reaction again causes an action. Karmas and samskaras (karmic traces) have, from the beginning, been inextricably linked to one another. But through Yoga we can free ourselves from this cycle. The fire of Yoga burns up karmas

Only when all the "seeds" of the Karmas and Vasanas (desires, wishes) have been roasted and burnt in the "fire of Yoga" can they no longer sprout. Only then does the door to liberation open to the aspirant. Because from then on one's actions produce no new samskaras in one's consciousness, and therefore no more effects for subsequent lives. With the dissolution of the ego – when the distinction of "I" and "you" no longer exist – the sanchit karma ((karma from earlier lives) also dissolves.

But the prarabdha karma (karma that has become "ripe" in this life and has already begun to work) is different. This continues to discharge itself. The following simile can serve as an example: When a turning wheel suddenly comes off, it continues to turn freely for a while before it finally comes to a standstill - this is how it is with karma. The root of birth and death – ignorance – is

Rudra Shivananda

in fact destroyed, but the plant (the present life) still exists for some time.

Self-Realization is not a "final state" – it is a new beginning. It is the end of our ignorance. It is the end of our childhood and as we grow in consciousness we should take up greater responsibilities. Whoever has acquired knowledge and experience through study applies this in their profession for the benefit of others. So it is also when someone has attained Unity Consciousness and knowledge through Samadhi, he or she should give to the rest of humanity.

Some Yogis withdraw from the activities of society and live as hermits far away from civilization. But they work spiritually for the benefit of the world through prayer and meditation. Their existence is itself a blessing for the world. Even the wind when it blows over the body of a jivanmukta is filled with Divine energy and radiation, and spreads harmony, happiness and peace everywhere it blows.

Other Realized Souls, though, go amongst people to teach them the truth. Even though they are liberated and unattached they give up the joy of vaikuntha (heaven) and return again to naraka (hell) in order to help living beings. To help others mentally and spiritually is a wonderful task – and at the same time a great art that requires deep understanding and comprehensive knowledge. For as long as we do not possess the insight and experience of a realized soul we should take care that we are not pulled back into Maya ourselves when we would like to help someone.

We are able to experience two types of Samadhi consciously -**savikalpa samadhi and nirvikalpa samadhi**

Savikalpa means "with movement (of the mind)". This type of samadhi is also known as sabija samadhi (with seed) and savichara samadhi (with differentiation). In savikalpa samadhi emotions, thoughts and desires still exist – partly conscious and partly as subconscious or unconscious karmic seeds. But in nirvikalpa samadhi (nirbija or nirvichara samadhi) no more thoughts whatsoever exist - not one "seed" of a desire or karma remains.

If we imagine a lake that is mirror-smooth and motionless, when a pebble is thrown into the water, circular ripples are created that reproduce and spread outwards. This represents every situation, every impression in our lives – 'waves' are produced in our minds, just as with the pebble thrown into the water, and these reproduce and spread in our consciousness. We cannot estimate just how much gravel and debris is submerged in our consciousness - that is why it can take such a long time for all disruptive factors (kleshas and vikshepas) to be raised, purified and cleared from the depths of our sub-consciousness. Once this happens and the mind again becomes still, we are able to advance to the Unity Consciousness.

The expression 'savikalpa samadhi' is related to sankalpa and vikalpa (a wish or resolution made and then dismissed). Just as a child builds a sandcastle, then soon afterwards destroys it and begins to build again, so in our imagination we create an entire world that we identify with and also experience. Then in the next moment when we come up with something else we destroy it – and so it continues non-stop.

To watch a child playing in the sand is entertaining and amusing for a short while. And so it is for a sage, a wise person, who watches with interest and is frequently astonished by how people seem to constantly build 'sandcastles' in their lives, and when one collapses to patiently begin to build the next.

Just as waking passes imperceptibly into sleep and sleep into dream, so we arrive at our first experience of savikalpa samadhi – inner enlightenment.

Enlightenment already begins in the agya chakra and the bindu chakra. The closer we come to the sahasara chakra, the more radiant the light becomes, until ultimately all forms dissolve and our inner space is filled with a radiant light, brighter than a thousand suns. We perceive a wonderful, all-pervasive sound (like the sound of OM sung by a thousand voices), and the door to the Infinite opens before our inner eye.

We all wish for spiritual experiences. But when the door of the sahasrara chakra opens for us we are like the swan ready to take flight, uncertain as to whether it should fly out into freedom or remain in the well-known surroundings. This is exactly how we feel when the Brahmarandhra opens. Even though this is what we have longed for and aimed at, it requires courage to take the next step when we are standing on the threshold.

It now lies with us whether we would like to continue with this experience or again withdraw to normal consciousness. For a seeker whose heart is filled with a burning desire for the divine light the meditation is not disturbed and continues.

The next level of samadhi is reached in the heavenly realms. On this level we can meet divine incarnations, liberated and God-Realized Saints and Masters. In line with our faith and the image of the Divine that we carry within us, each of us has different visions and experiences at this level of samadhi. Though, generally, it means that we have reached a heavenly sphere where we are joyfully welcomed. Here we can have many beautiful experiences. We meet the divine masters and return again to the 'normal' world with wisdom and knowledge.

Savikalpa samadhi brings us wonderful 'heavenly' experiences. Afterwards we can almost become addicted to them. But, gradually it becomes clear to us that we are unable to attain liberation in this way as we are still moving in other levels of consciousness. Then we again begin to strive for Realization and are finally guided to nirvikalpa samadhi.

Nirvikalpa samadhi is the state of pure bliss and absolute peace. It is not possible to describe this state as it is beyond all descriptions. In this state, the jivatma quenches its lifelong thirst for fulfillment in unit with the Atma. It releases itself from the limitations of individuality and merges with the divine Self, the supreme Consciousness. It experiences itself as the "center" of the Universe – as Atma, the spirit.

There is no suffering, no pain and no problems in the Divine Consciousness – everything is perfect (purna). There are no wishes, no longing – no knower, no object and no knowledge; neither time nor space. There is only undivided existence – pure Being. The identification with the individual person and individuality dissolves in the all-encompassing Self.

Many people maintain that someone who has attained nirvikalpa samadhi, and therefore moksha, cannot live much longer. However, it is said that there are two types of realization. Some experience God-Realization (Atma Gyana) with full consciousness and continue to live afterwards as a jivanmukta (realized and liberated soul) in order to pass their knowledge on. Others, however, experience enlightenment and liberation only when they leave the body. Qualitatively there is no difference. Those who attain Moksha at the end of their mortal life are liberated and realized in the same way as those who have attained God-Realization during their earthly existence.

Nirvikalpa Samadhi is a state of indescribable happiness, from which we no longer want to return, and from where we can see no reason whatsoever why we should come back. We are everywhere – there is no place where we need to go. Who should return? From where, and to where?

Nevertheless many decide to bring their consciousness back into the body. Out of pure mercy they voluntarily renounce remaining in the bliss of samadhi consciousness, and stay in the world to help innumerable souls who are still in the sorrowful condition of ignorance.

The liberated ones are forever free from the chains of karma, which also means they are no longer subject to the cycle of birth and death. All the same, a few of them continue to return to the earth of their own free will - their only goal is to help other beings to attain liberation - only one who is free can free others.

Considerations for
3rd Level Sadhana

In the following pages, I will be including a whole lot of mantras that may be suited for your third level practice. However, it is important to keep in mind:

1. It is necessary to be initiated properly into the mantra. If you cannot find a mantra Master, keep doing the 2nd level practice unitl one appears. Have confidence that when you are ready, the guide will appear.

2. It is good to be familiar with the range of mantras so that when the guide appears, you may already have the right mantra in your heart. Otherwise, ask the guide to provide one.

3. Although only the main mantra is given, please be aware that there should be a sadhana associated with it - similar to the 2nd level sadhanas. However, if your guide decides that the mantra alone is sufficient, then make sure that it is unlocked or you are given the key.

4. Mantra practice can be deepened by the following:

    - With awareness of breath
    - Breath is forgotten
    - Penetration of mind
    - Mantra repeats itself
    - Stillness - no mind, only awareness

5. Be aware if of the quality of the mind - the different states:

    - Turbulent - unrestrained
    - Distracted - some level of control
    - Controlled - no distractions
    - Stupefied
    - Ekagra or one-pointed

6. Different ways of integrating the mantra into your life:

    - Mantra with awareness of breath
    - Mantra while performing daily tasks
    - Listening to mantra at heart center
    - Practicing mantra with spinal breathing
    - Merging mantra into bindu of chakra
    - Taking the mantra into the heart space
    - Taking the mantra into the third-eye

7. Degrees of mantra practice:
    - Vaikhari - aloud: not recommended for level 3
    - Madhyama - mental
    - Pashyanti - vibration
    - Paravak – supreme absorption

Proper Use of Mala for Mantra Practice

In the 2nd and 3rd level sadhanas, it is necessary to practice repetition the main mantra 108 times.

Whether you have been initiated into a mantra practice or enjoying some mantra from an audio CD or even a book, if you are serious about practicing, you would need to use a mala or a rosary of one hundred and eight beads. The mala is used for counting the number of repetitions of the specific mantra. A practice generally requires the repetition of 108 counts or a multiple of 108 per session, with an ultimate goal of reaching a certain number such as 108,000 or 144,000 or even 1,080,000.

Since the mala is such an important tool in mantra practice, over the generations a large body of mystique has arisen over its proper use. A lot of the lore may be questionable, but much is quite symbolic as well as practical.

To understand some of the guidelines, it is necessary keep in mind that it is basic to the mystique of the mala that the beads retain some of the power and energy from the mantra itself. This means that the mala becomes a storage medium for mantric power and energy – this is especially true for one made from the rudraksha beads.

There are some practitioners who actually hide their malas under a bag as they count out the repetitions so as to prevent others from "stealing" their energy. This is somewhat extreme and most practitioners need not worry about such an event occurring.

I would recommend the following cautionary guidelines:

1. Use a bag to hold your mala rather than just putting it into your pockets as it will easily get damaged from frequent taking in and out or even get inadvertently lost.

2. Do not wear the mala that you are using for mantra practice as your body will then re-absorb the energy. If one wishes to wear a mala, it should be a separate one used only for wearing.
3. Never drop the mala on the floor or let someone else handle it as that will drain the energy.
4. Hold the mala with your second and third /ring fingers and do not touch it with the first finger as it is considered to have egoistic energy.
5. When you finish one round of 108 and wish to continue another round, do not go over the head bead which is not counted – one should flip the mala over and go back the way you had come.
6. If you are practicing more than one mantra, it is better to use a separate mala for the second mantra – best not to mix mantras on one mala.
7. If you mala bets broken and the beads are separated, do not try to mend it, but retire it away in a bag under you alter. A broken mala can no longer hold the energy and also may have an negative effect on your mantric practice.
8. The left hand is not used for mantric practice.
9. If you cannot complete the mala at some session, you can use a pin to clip the location where you stopped, and continue from there when you have time – you do not need to start all over again.
10. Only a rudrasksha mala can be used for Shiva mantras or Shakti mantras – do not use crystal or lotus or some other material.

Try to get the best quality mala that you can as a low quality one will easily break during you practice. Smaller beads are used for mantra practice while malas with large beads are only used for wearing.

Shakti Bija mantras

These are single-syllable mantras which can consist of several vowels or consonants used for projecting cosmic energies such as prana, energies of Sun, Moon, Electricity, Magnetism and fire. They can hold, resonate and transform these Divine Mother energies including Kundalini shakti.

The "ee" sound is the primal sound of Shakti while the consonant "r" has the seed sound of fire and light. Those that contain the consonant "l" provide for the seed of earth and stabilization. Those that have the h-sound project prana while those s or sh sound uses the moon energy to affect the mind.

The following are some of the major bija mantras:

OM and *AUM*
This is the mother of all mantras. Om is the basic vibration of the universe. Repeating it brings us closer to our true Self – the Purusha or the Atman. On the microcosmic level, our energies move up the spine and enhances higher prana, making Om repetition a great way to start a meditation or spiritual practice. Aum is an expansion of Om and gives stronger power. A is the sound of Brahma the creator, U is that of Vishnu the preserver and M is the sound of Lord Shiva.

HAUM
In this mantra, Ha is Shiva and au is Sadashiva. The nada and bindu mean that which dispels sorrow. With this mantra, the

power of Lord Shiva is invoked.

DUM

Here Da means Durga, and u means to protect. Nada means Mother of the universe, and bindu signifies action (worship or prayer). This is the bija mantra of Durga.

KREEM

With this mantra Kalika should be worshipped. Ka is Kali, ra is Brahman, and ee is Mahamaya. Nada is the Mother of the universe, and bindu is the dispeller of sorrow.

HREEM

This is the mantra of Mahamaya or Bhuvaneshwaree. Ha means Shiva, ra is Prakriti, ee means Mahamaya. Nada is the Mother of the universe, and bindu is the dispeller of sorrow.

SHREEM

This is the mantra of Maha Lakshmée. Sha is Maha Lakshme, ra means wealth. Ee is satisfaction or contentment. Nada is the manifested Brahman, and bindu is the dispeller of sorrow.

AIM

This is the bija mantra of Saraswati. Ai stands for Saraswati, and bindu is the dispeller of sorrow.

KLEEM

This is the Kama bija mantra. Ka means Kama deva, the Lord of desire; it also means Lord Krishna. La means Indra, the ruler of Heaven, also lord of the senses. Ee means contentment or satisfaction. Nada and bindu mean those that bring happiness and sorrow.

HUM

In this mantra Ha is Shiva, and U is Bhairava. Nada is the Supreme, and bindu means dispeller of sorrow.

GAM

This is the Ganesha bija mantra. Ga means Ganesha, and Bindu is the dispeller of sorrow. "Gam" is the ekakshara mantra of Ganapati. This is called Ganapati bija mantra as well. Atharva Sheersh (Atharva Sanhitaa) mention it as Ganapati bija and for the Sadhana of this single lettered Mantra there is a procedure laid down in Agama and Tantra Shastra with a separate dhyan and parivara devata. The dhyaan and ang devataa are different than Maha Ganapati for ekaakshara mantra .

GLAUM

This is also a mantra of Ganesha. Ga means Ganesha, la means that which pervades, au means luster or brilliance, and bindu is the dispeller of sorrow.

KSHRAUM

This is the bija mantra of Narasinha Bhagavan, a very fierce half-man half-lion incarnation of Lord Vishnu. Ksha is Narasinh, ra is Brahma, au means with teeth pointing upwards, and bindu means dispeller of sorrow.

AM

This bija mantra is for Agni deva. When Agni deva is worshipped, the mantra with the bija is chanted as follows: "Om Am Aagnaye Namah"

VAM

The Mantra Vam is the Amrita mantra mainly ascribed to Varuna and it is used for the amriteekaran in arghya sthaapanaa. It is also used as part of bhoot shuddhi.

Figure 11

Divine Mother Gayatri
Embodiment of Light

Gayatri Mantras

Gayatri Mantras are very powerful meditation aids to pray for the grace of a particular God. Gayatri (गायत्री) is the feminine form of gāyatra, a Sanskrit word for a song or a hymn. It may refer to a mantra in particular (attributed to Vishwamitra - goddess as its personification - represents Parabrahman) or the name of a Vedic poetic meter of 24 syllables (three lines of eight syllables each) or any hymn composed in this meter.

Gayatri Devi Mantra

ॐ भूर्भुवस्वः ।
तत् सवितुर्वरेण्यं ।
भर्गो देवस्य धीमहि ।
धियो यो नः प्रचोदयात् ॥

Om bhur bhuvah svah
Tat savitur vareniyam
Bhargo devasya dhimahi
Dhiyo yo nah prachodayat.

Om, Almighty Supreme Sun
Impel us with your divine brilliance
So that we may attain a noble understanding of Reality.

Durga Gayatri Mantra

Om Kathyayanaya Vidhmahe
Kanya Kumari cha Dheemahe
Thanno Durgaya Prachodayath.

Om, Let me meditate on the goddesswho is daughter of
Kathyayana,
Oh, maiden Goddess, give me higher intellect,
And let Goddess Durga illuminate my mind.

Lakshmi Gayatri Mantra

Om Mahadevyaicha Vidhmahe
Vishnu Pathniyaicha Dheemahe
Thanno Lakshmi Prachodayath.

Om, Let me meditate on the greatest goddess,
Oh, wife of Lord Vishnu, give me higher intellect,
And let Goddess Lakshmi illuminate my mind.

Saraswathi Gayatri Mantra

Om Vakdeviyai cha Vidhmahe
Virinji Pathniyai cha Dheemahe
Thanno Vani Prachodayath.

Rudra Shivananda

Om, Let me meditate on the goddess of speech,
Oh, wife of Lord Brahma, give me higher intellect,
And let Goddess Vani illuminate my mind.

Sita Gayatri Mantra

Om Janaka Nandinye Vidhmahe
Bhumijayai Dheemahe
Thanno Sita Prachodayath .

Om, Let me meditate on the daughter of Janaka
Oh, daughter of earth, give me higher intellect,
And let Sita illuminate my mind.

Radha Gayatri Mantra

Om Vrishabhanujaye Vidhmahe
Krishna priyaya Dheemahe
Thanno Radha Prachodayath.

Om, Let me meditate on the daughter of Vrishabhanu,
Oh, darling of Krishna, give me higher intellect,
And let Radha illuminate my mind.

Shiva Gayatri

Om Tat Purushaya Vidhmahe
Mahadevaya Dheemahe
Thanno Rudra Prachodayath.

Om, Let me meditate on the great Purusha,

Oh, greatest God, give me higher intellect,
And let God Rudra illuminate my mind.

Narayana Gayatri Mantra

Om Narayanaya Vidhmahe
Vasudevaya Dheemahe
Thanno Vishnu Prachodayath.

Om, Let me meditate on Lord Narayana,
Oh, Lord Vasudeva, give me higher intellect,
And let Lord Vishnu illuminate my mind.

Rama Gayatri Mantra

Om Daserathaya Vidhmahe
Sita Vallabhaya Dheemahe
Thanno Rama Prachodayath.

Om, Let me meditate on the son of Dasaratha,
Oh, consort of Sita, give me higher intellect,
And let God Rama illuminate my mind.

Krishna Gayatri Mantra

Om Dhamodharaya Vidhmahe
Rukmani Vallabhay Dheemahe
Thanno Krishna Prachodayath.

Om, Let me meditate on the god whose belly was tied by a rope,
Oh, consort of Rukhmani, give me higher intellect,

And let God Krishna illuminate my mind.

Om Govindaya Vidhmahe
Gopi Vallabhaya Dheemahe
Thanno Krishna Prachodayath .

Om, Let me meditate on the god who takes care of all beings,
Oh, darling of all gopis, give me higher intellect,
And let God Krishna illuminate my mind.

Venkateswara Gayatri Mantra

Nirnajanaya Vidmahe
Nirapasaya Dheemahe
Thanno Srinivasa Prachodayath.

Om, Let me meditate on the god who is eternal truth,
Oh, God who does not have attachments, give me higher
intellect,
And let God Srinivasa illuminate my mind.

Narasimha Gayatri Mantra

Om Narasimhaya Vidmahe
Vajra Nakhaya Dheemahe
Thanno Narasimha Prachodayath.

Om, Let me meditate on the god who is the lion man,
Oh, God who has diamond claws, give me higher intellect,
And let God Narasimha illuminate my mind.

Hayagreeva Gayatri Mantra

Om Vanisvaraya Vidhmahe
Hayagrivaya Dhimahi
Tanno Hayagriva Pracodayat.

Om, Let me meditate on the god of learning,
Oh, God who has a horse face, give me higher intellect,
And let God Hayagreeva illuminate my mind.

Sudharshana Gayatri Mantra

Om Sudharshanaya Vidmahe
Maha Jwalaya Dheemahe
Thanno Chakra Prachodayath.

Om, Let me meditate on the holy wheel of Sudharshana,
Oh, Wheel which has great brilliance, give me higher intellect,
And let the wheel illuminate my mind.

Brahma Gayatri Mantra

Om Chathur mukhaya Vidmahe
Hamasaroodaya Dheemahe
Thanno Brahma Prachodayath.

Om, Let me meditate on the God with four faces,
Oh, God who rides on the Swan, give me higher intellect,
And let the Lord Brahma illuminate my mind.

Om Vedathmanaya vidmahe,
Hiranya Garbhaya Dheemahi,
Thanno Brahma prachodayath

Om, Let me meditate on the God who is the soul of Vedas,
Oh God, who holds the entire world within you, give me higher intellect,
And let the Lord Brahma illuminate my mind.

Ganesha Gayatri Mantra [1]

Om Lambhodaraya vidmahe
Mahodaraya deemahi
Thanno danthi prachodayath.

Om, Let me meditate on that god with broad paunch
Oh, God with a big belly, give me higher intellect,
And let the elephant faced one illuminate my mind.

Ganesha Gayatri Mantra [2]

Om Ekadanthaya vidmahe
Vakrathundaya dheemahi
Thanno danthi prachodayath.

Om, Let me meditate on that one tusked God,
Oh, God with broken tusk, give me higher intellect,
And let the elephant faced one illuminate my mind.

Ganesha Gayatri Mantra [3]

Om Thatpurashaya vidhmahe
Vakrathundaya dheemahi
Thanno danthi prachodayath.

Om, Let me meditate on that great male,
Oh, God with broken tusk, give me higher intellect,
And let the elephant faced one illuminate my mind.

Subrahamanya Gayatri Mantra

Om That Purushaya Vidhmahe
Maha Senaya Dheemahe
Thanno Shanmuga Prachodayath.

Om, Let me meditate on that great male,
Oh, commander in chief, give me higher intellect,
And let the six faced one illuminate my mind.

Devendra Gayatri Mantra

Om Sahasra nethrayeVidhmahe
Vajra hasthaya Dheemahe
Thanno Indra Prachodayath.

Om, Let me meditate on the thousand eyed one,
Oh, Lord with Vajra as weapon, give me higher intellect,
And let Indra illuminate my mind.

Hanuman Gayatri Mantra

Om Aanjaneya Vidhmahe
Maha balaya Dheemahe
Thanno Hanuman Prachodayath.

Om, Let me meditate on the son of Anjana,
Oh, Very strong one, give me higher intellect,
And let Hanuman illuminate my mind.

Om Aanjaneya Vidhmahe
Vayu puthraya Dheemahe
Thanno Hanuman Prachodayath .

Om, Let me meditate on the son of Anjana,
Oh, son of god of air, give me higher intellect,
And let Hanuman illuminate my mind.

Aadithya [Sun] Gayatri Mantra

Om Bhaskaraya Vidhmahe
Diva karaya Dheemahe
Thanno Surya Prachodayath.

Om, Let me meditate on the Sun God,
Oh, maker of the day, give me higher intellect,
And let Sun God illuminate my mind.

Om Aswadwajaya Vidhmahe
Pasa Hasthaya Dheemahe
Thanno Surya Prachodayath .

Figure 12

The Lord Surya
The Power of the Sun

Om, Let me meditate on the god who has a horse flag,
Oh, God who holds the rope, give me higher intellect,
And let Sun God illuminate my mind.

Chandra [Moon] Gayatri Mantra

Om Kshira puthraya Vidhmahe
Amrithathvaya Dheemahe
Thanno Chandra Prachodayath.

Om, Let me meditate on the son of milk,
Oh, essence of nectar, give me higher intellect,
And let moon God illuminate my mind.

Om Padmadwajaya Vidhmahe
Hema roopaya Dheemahe
Thanno Chandra Prachodayath .

Om, Let me meditate on God who has lotus in his flag,
Oh, God of golden colour, give me higher intellect,
And let moon God illuminate my mind.

Angaaraka (Mars) Gayatri Mantra

Om veeradhwajaaya vidmahae
vighna hastaaya dheemahi
tanno bhouma prachodayaat

Om, Let me meditate on him who has hero in his flag,
Oh, He who has power to solve problems, give me higher
intellect,
And let the son of earth God illuminate my mind.

Budha (Mercury) Gayatri Mantra

Om gajadhwajaaya vidmahae
sukha hastaaya dheemahi
tanno budha: prachodayaat

Om, Let me meditate on him who has elephant in his flag,
Oh, He who has power to grant pleasure, give me higher
intellect,
And let Budha illuminate my mind.

Guru (Jupiter) Gayatri Mantra

Om vrishabadhwajaaya vidmahae
kruni hastaaya dheemahi
tanno guru: prachodayaat

Om, Let me meditate on him who has bull in his flag,
Oh, He who has power to get things done, give me higher
intellect,
And let Guru illuminate my mind.

Shukra (Venus) Gayatri Mantra

Om aswadhwajaaya vidmahae
dhanur hastaaya dheemahi
tanno shukra: prachodayaat

Om, Let me meditate on him who has horse in his flag,
Oh, He who has a bow in his hand, give me higher intellect,
And let Shukra illuminate my mind.

Shanishwara (Saturn) Gayatri Mantra

*Om kaakadhwajaaya vidmahae
khadga hastaaya dheemahi
tanno mandah: prachodayaat*

Om, Let me meditate on him who has crow in his flag,
Oh, He who has a sword in his hand, give me higher intellect,
And let Saneeswara illuminate my mind.

Raahu Gayatri Mantra

*om naakadhwajaaya vidmahae
padma hastaaya dheemahi
tanno raahu: prachodayaat*

Om, Let me meditate on him who has snake in his flag,
Oh, He who has a lotus in his hand, give me higher intellect,
And let Rahu illuminate my mind.

Ketu Gayatri Mantra

*om aswadhwajaaya vidmahae
soola hastaaya dheemahi
tanno ketu: prachodayaat*

Om, Let me meditate on him who has horse in his flag,
Oh, He who has a trident in his hand, give me higher intellect,
And let Kethu illuminate my mind.

Yama Gayatri Mantra

Om Surya puthraya Vidhmahe
Maha Kalaya Dheemahe
Thanno Yama Prachodayath.

Om, Let me meditate on the son of Sun God,
Oh, great Lord of time, give me higher intellect,
And let God of death illuminate my mind.

Varuna Gayatri Mantra

Om Jala bimbhaya Vidhmahe
Nila Purushaya Dheemahe
Thanno Varuna Prachodayath.

Om, Let me meditate on the reflection of water,
Oh, person of ocean blue, give me higher intellect,
And let the God of water illuminate my mind.

Agni Gayatri Mantra

Om Maha jwalaya Vidhmahe
Agni devaya Dheemahe
Thanno Agni Prachodayath.

Om, Let me meditate on the great flame,
Oh, God of fire, give me higher intellect,
And let the Fire God illuminate my mind.

Rudra Shivananda

Om Vaiswanaraya Vidhmahe
Laaleelaya Dheemahe
Thanno Agni Prachodayath .

Om, Let me meditate on the flame that digests,
Oh, merger of all, give me higher intellect,
And let the Fire God illuminate my mind.

Prithvi Gayatri Mantra

Om Prithivi devyyaya Vidhmahe
Sahasra murthaye cha Dheemahe
Thanno Prithvi Prachodayath.

Om, Let me meditate on the goddess of earth,
Oh, Goddess who has thousand forms, give me higher intellect,
And let Goddess earth illuminate my mind.

Garuda Gayatri Mantra

Om Thathpurushaya Vidhmahe
Suvarna Pakshaya Dheemahe
Thanno Garuda Prachodayath .

Om, Let me meditate on that great living being,
Oh, Bird with golden wings, give me higher intellect,
And let the God Garuda illuminate my mind

Nandi Gayatri Mantra

Om Thathpurushaya Vidhmahe
Chakrathundaya Dheemahe
Thanno Nandi Prachodayath .

Om, Let me meditate on that great living being,
Oh, Lord of devas, give me higher intellect,
And let the God Nandi illuminate my mind

Tulasi Gayatri Mantra

Om Tulasi devyai cha Vidhmahe
Vishnu priyayai cha Dheemahe
Thanno Brindah Prachodayath.

Om, Let me meditate on the Goddess of Ocimum,
Oh, Goddess who is dear to Vishnu, give me higher intellect,
And let Brindha* illuminate my mind.
* Another name for Thulasi plant

Shirdi Sai Gayatri Mantra

Om Shirdi vasaya Vidhmahe
Sachithanandaya Dheemahe
Thanno Sai Prachodayath .

Om, Let me meditate on the God who lives in Shirdi,
Oh, God who is the ethereal truth and happiness, give me higher
intellect,
And let that Sai illuminate my mind.

Deva/Devi Mantras

There are countless mantras to invoke the power of the devas and many are used to connect with their power to attain to liberation. The following is a selection:

Lord Shiva

Om Nama Shivaya

Om Haum Jum Saha

Mahamrityunjaya Mantra

Aum Triyambakam Yajamahe

Sugandhim Pushti Vardhanam

Urvarukam Iva Bandhanane

Mrityor Mukshiye Mamritat

Figure 13

Lord Shiva
The Universal Consciousness Being

Lord Shiva is the lord of yoga and is the enigmatic power that enables all mortal beings snared in the grips of karma to overcome all the obstacles that prevent Self-Realization.

In the microcosm, he is the power that dissolves our illusionary ego and desires. In the macrocosm, he is the destroyer of the universe at the end of time and enables the rebirth of a new universe.

Figure 14
Mahamrityunjaya
An Aspect of Lord Shiva

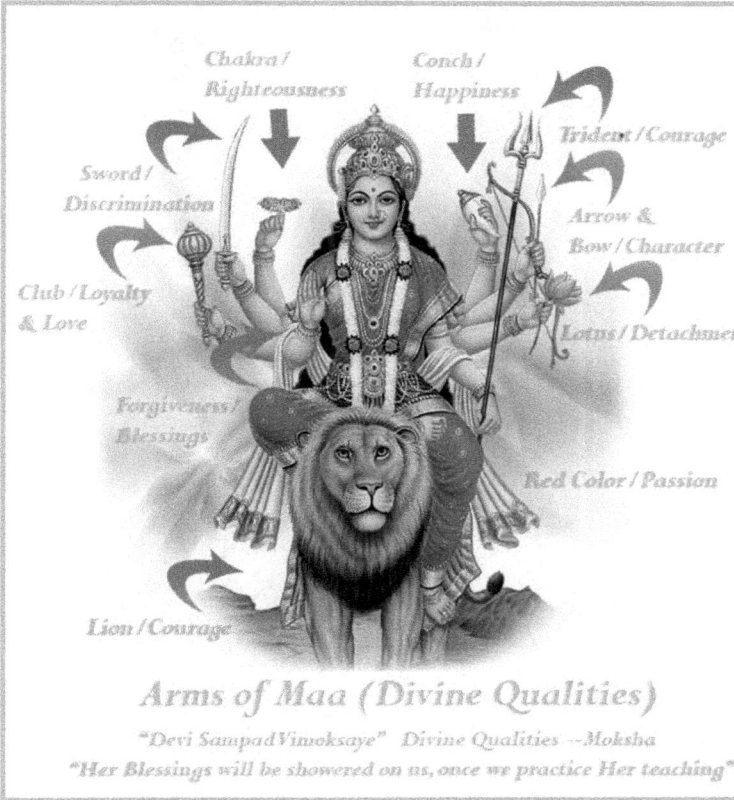

Chakra / Righteousness

Conch / Happiness

Trident / Courage

Sword / Discrimination

Arrow & Bow / Character

Club / Loyalty & Love

Lotus / Detachment

Forgiveness / Blessings

Red Color / Passion

Lion / Courage

Arms of Maa (Divine Qualities)

"*Devi Sampad Vimoksaye*" *Divine Qualities --Moksha*

"*Her Blessings will be showered on us, once we practice Her teaching*"

Figure 15
Mother Durga
Emodiment of the Power to Destroy Negativity

Mother Durga Mantras

Om Dum Durgaya Namaha

Aum Aing Hring Kling Chamundaye Vichchey Namaha

[141]

Figure 16
Lord Rama
The Incarnarnation of Righteousmess and Duty

Lord Rama Mantra

Shri Rama, Jai Rama, Jai Jai Rama

Figure 17
Lord Krishna
The Incarnation of Love

Lord Krishna Mantras

Om Klim Krishnaye Namaha

Om Namo Bhagavate Vasudevaya

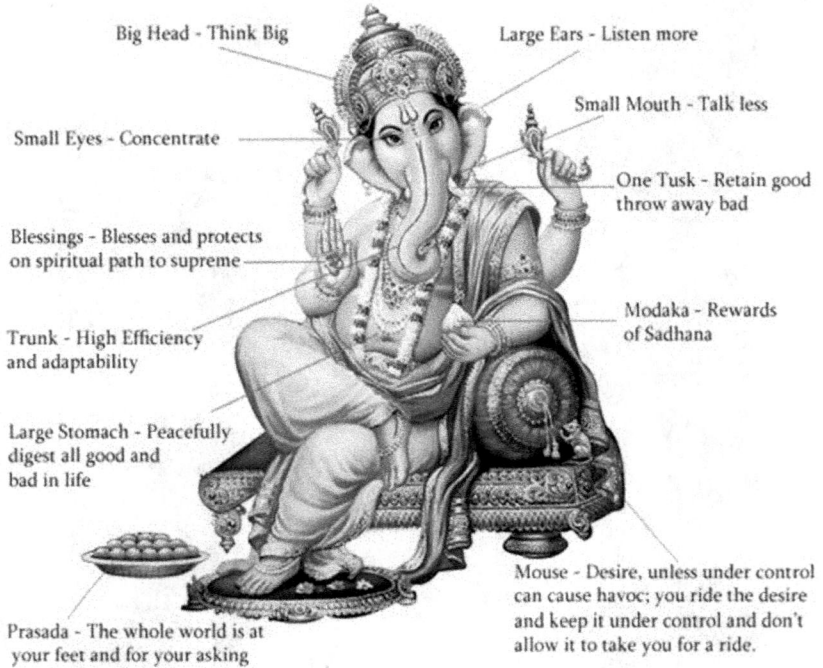

Figure 18
Lord Ganesh
Lord of the World - Wisdom
[For more information, read page]

Lord Ganesha Mantras

Om Gam Ganeshaya Namaha

Om Gam Ganapataye Namaha

Figure 19
Lord Skanda
Lord of Battle and Spirituality

Lord Skanda Mantra

Om Sharavana Bhava

Rudra Shivananda

Figure 20

Lord Hanuman

The Power of Life-force and Devotion

Lord Hanuman Mantra

Om Ham Hanumate Namaha

Figure 21

Mother Lakshmi

The Power of Prosperity & Success

Mother Laksmi Mantra

Aum Shring Hring Kling MahaLakshmaye Namaha

Figure 22

Markandeya - Seer of Mahamrityunjaya

Stories for 3rd Level Mantras

Many of the major mantras have some backstory to illustrate its nature and how the mantra was received. For some of the deity mantras, additional information is useful in order to connect better with the divine power.

Markandeya and Mrityunjaya

In ages past, there was an old couple who were kind and loved by one and all. However, they were secretly unhappy because they had no son. The old man, Mrikandu Munivar worshipped Shiva and sought from him the boon of begetting a son. He was given the choice between a sage with a short life on earth or a mediocre person with a long life. The couple agreed to chose the former, and was blessed with Markandeya, an exemplary son, destined to die at the age of sixteen.

Markandeya grew up to be a great devotee of Lord Shiva. He would travel to visit great yogis and discuss universal mysteries and truths with them. No matter where he was, every morning, after taking his bath, he would perform the worship of Lord Shiva in the form of the Shivalingam – a representation of the consciousness of the universe.

On the day of his destined death, his sixteenth birthday, Markandeya was traveling back home from another sage's hermitage. As he began his worship of Lord Shiva, the representatives of Lord Yama, the Power of Death, came to take the youth's soul, but were repulsed by the divine light surrounding him during his devotion.

The minions of Death reported the situation and Yama himself came in person to take the youth's life away. At this time, Markandeya was suddenly filled with a great dread of death, and spontaneously drew from the Divine, the great Mrityunjaya mantra and started to recite it. This mantra entreated Lord Shiva to save one from an untimely death among other blessings. When Death sprung his noose around the young sage's neck, it accidentally landed around the Shivalingam – Yama had never missed before. Shiva emerged in all his fury, and kicked Yama and killed Death itself.

The youth thanked the Lord but then entreated Him to revive Death as the death of Death would upset the world order. Lord Shiva then revived Death, but obtained his promise that the devout youth would live for ever. Another title for Lord Shiva is Mrityunjaya.

Markandeya is the seer of the Mrityunjaya mantra which saves those who recite it from untimely death. From a spiritual perspective, it can help strengthen all our positive qualities and bring more light into our lives to destroy all negative qualities.

While the day you are going to die may be pre-destined, it can be changed, but only you can change it. You yourself can bring forward the day when you are going to die through pursuing injurious habits such as drugs or smoking or even suicide, or you yourself can extend your life by earnestly expressing the demand for this extension to the Divine.

aum mrityunjaya mahādeva trāhi mām śaranāgatam
janmamityujarāvyādhi pīditam karmabandhanai

Aum, O Great Lord Mrityuñjaya, I take refuge in You, Protect me;
And relieve me of the painful experiences of birth, death, old-age and disease.

Lord Ganesha – Overcoming Obstacles

One of the most intriguing of all the Divine cosmic forces that can come to our aid is that of Lord Ganesha. The elephant-headed son of Lord Shiva is called Ganapati, the Lord of the ganas or heavenly host; Vinayaka, the Supreme Leader; and also as Vighneshvara, or the Lord of Obstacles. These names indicate that He is the master of the circumstances that obstruct any path and with His help, all obstacles can be overcome. This is why all auspicious acts and rituals are undertaken with His invocation first.

From a yogic point of view, Lord Ganesha as the Lord of the physical world represented by the first energy center or muladhara chakra, helps to overcome all external physical, emotional and mental obstacles.

The form of Lord Ganesha is very symbolic and it can be very instructive for us to learn more about it:

1. The large head of an elephant is necessary to hold all the knowledge that is in the universe. The elephant is also a symbol of wisdom and of long memory.
2. The big ears are for listening to scriptures and to hear our pleas for help.
3. The trunk is a very versatile instrument – it can be used to lift heavy objects or a fine blade of grass. Our intellect should be able to be so efficient that we can solve all the problems, big or small that occur in our lives.
4. There are two tusks to indicate that we should be able to differentiate between good or evil, right or wrong, real or

unreal. However, one tusk is broken to indicate that we should grow out of the world of relativity based on pairs of opposites to achieve unity.

5. His vehicle is a mouse which represents desire – it is very small but capable of much damage if not under control. The mouse looks at the food placed before Lord Ganesha, but does not eat without His permission.
6. In one hand He holds a rope which is used to pull us towards Him, while in a second hand, He holds an axe to cut off our harmful desires. In a third hand, he holds a sweet rice ball to reward those that reach towards Him and in the fourth hand, He blesses them.
7. In a side view, He has the outline of the Sanskrit character of OM – the essential vibration of the universe.

The following is a mantra for invoking his presence and blessings:

Suklaambaradaram Vishnum
Shashi-varnam Caturghujham
Prasanna vadanam dhyaayet
Sarva vighnopa Shantayet.

I meditate on Lord Ganesha, who wears white garments and is all-pervading
Whose color is that of the moon, who is four-armed
Whose face is always peaceful and happy
I meditate on Him who removes all obstacles.

More about Keelakam

All great mantras or stotras are recognized within two different purposes – (a) *Loukika mantra*, and (b) *Moksha mantra*. The Loukika mantra is composed to help the devotee to seek blessings from the deity to fulfill desires, while the Moksha mantra is meant to lead towards unity with the Divine. Some prayers are intertwined with both purposes.

The Keelakam or linchpin is the very important and strategic large nail that holds the cartwheel in place on the central axle of a vehicle. It requires extraordinary strength, and one has to have absolute faith in its ability to provide the support for the journey. One knows that the linchpin will not betray the vehicle.

An example is the Sri Ram Raksha Stotra which serves as a vehicle on the journey to Rama, the eighth avatar of Lord Vishnu. The sage-poet Shri Buddha Kousika Rishi recognizes Lord Hanuman as the fulcrum who would give the absolutely reliable strength in the journey. In the introductory prelude, he says that the stotra is in the form of a mantra (asya Sri Rama raksha stotra mantrasya). The deity of the stotra is Shri Sitaram, i.e., Sita's Ram (Sri Sitaramachandro Devata). It is written in the Anushtup Chanda, and the power to the stotra is derived from Sita (Sita Shaktihi), and that Shri Hanuman is the crucial fulcrum in the form of the linchpin that holds the cartwheel (Srimad Hanuman Keelakam).

Rudra Shivananda

In the Sri Rama Raksha Stotra, the sage-poet Sri Budha Kousika Rishi specifies the framework by explaining in proper sequence, as it should be. Most stotras and mantras are composed in the sequence of – (a) Rishi = naming the author, e.g. Sri Budha Kousika Rishi, (b) Chanda = specifying the metre of the verse, e.g. Anushtup Chanda, (c) Devatha = identifying the deity, e.g. Sita's Ramachandra, (d) Shakti = explaining the source of strength to the stotra, e.g. Sita, and (e) Keelakam = locating the fulcrum or linchpin, e.g. Hanuman.

The sequence varies in some mantras or stotras, where the *Beejam* (= seed) is also identified. In such prayers, the sequence is – Rishi – Chanda – Devatha – Beejam – Keelakam – Shakti.

The recognition of the status of the keelakam is found in most mantras and stotras. There are complex prayers that are known to be crucial in seeking the blessings of the multiple aspect s of various deities. The entire prayer in such examples are classified as 'keelakam' and are to be recited accordingly – Devi Keelakam, Keelakam Stotram or the Vishnu Sahasranaama Keelakam.

The prayer to Devi, the 'Durga Saptasati' is one of the most complex dhyaana stotras, comprising nearly 700 slokas or verses. The entire sequence separated into different 'chapters', if one may term them as such. However, all the chapters comprising the entire range of 700 slokas are hinged on the earlier Keelakam Sloka, being the fulcrum. The Durga Saptasati has a verse that is very commonly recited by most devotees in prayer, to Devi, but rarely does anyone place it in the sequence of the 700 slokas.

Sarva mangala mangalye,
Sive sarvaartha saadike,

Sharanye tryambake Gowri,
Narayani namosthuthe

Thirteen chapters follow the Keelakam Sloka, and the devotee is usually advised to recite the verses over an entire week.

When one crosses over from the stotra to the aspects of tantra or mantra, the position of the Keelakam is extremely specific and elaborate. The Keelakam is not mentioned merely in passing, but placed in the sequence of prayer, with deliberate instructions to the devotee. This is true of the Sri Sri Chandi.

The Keelakam in the prayers and recitation of the Sri Sri Chandi, follows the (a) Devi Suktam, (b) Kavacham, and (c) Araghala Stotram, similar to the Durga Saptasati. The Keelakam is followed by the (d) Ratri Suktam, (e) Devi Mahatmya, (f) Phala Sruti and, (g) Kshama Prarthana. Rishi Markandeya has recited the Keelakam in sixteen slokas in this prayer.

A third example is Shiva Kavacham as presented in the Skanda Purana. The rishi Rishabha Deva taught the Shiva Kavacham to Bhadraayu.

Asya Shiva Kavacha Stotra Mahamantrasya
Brahma Rishi, Anushtup Chanda,
Sri Sada Shivo Rudro Devatha, Hreem Shakti,
Ram Keelakam, Sreem, Hreem, Kleem Bheejam,
Sri Sada Shivapreetyarthe,
Shiva Kavacha Stotra Jape Viniyogaha

The Shiva Kavacham presents the sequence of – (a) Rishi = Brahma, (b) Chanda = Anushtup, (c) Devatha = Sada Shiva Rudra, (d) Shakti = Hreem, (e) Keelakam = Rama, (f) Bheejam

= Sreem, Hreem, Kleem. There is another version, wherein the Rishi is Rishabha Yogeeshwara Rishi, Bheejam is 'Om', and Keelakam is 'Shiva'.

A fourth example is The Sri Hanuman Kavacham Stotram. It is in the form of the dialogue between Shiva and Parvati. Upon an enquiry by Parvati – How can people be protected from sorrow? "Kena raksha bhaved dhruvam?" From fear of the dead, the fire of the funeral pyre and sorrow?

Shiva recites, in response, the guidance provided by Rama to Vibheeshana, and specifies that the reciting of the Sri Hanuman Kavacham Stotram would be the only pathway to seek strength and support in times of distress from sorrows that cannot be reversed.

Om Asya Sri Hanuman Kavacha Stotra Maha Mantrasya,
Sri Ramachandra Rishi,
Sri Hanuman Parmarthma Devatha,
Anushtup Chanda,
Maruthaatmaja Ithi Bheeja Anjanaa Soorithi Sakthi,
Lakshmana Prana Ithi Keelakam...

The Keelakam in this stotra is the aspect of giving life to Lakshmana by Hanuman, and the recitation of the Sri Hanuman Kavaca Stotram is to give encouragement and courage to the devotee under duress or sorrow, sometimes due to the loss of a close relative, or the extended distress due to illness.

Although in the above strotras and mantras, the keelakam is explicitly given, there are other cases where it serves as a key to unlock powerful mantras. The great sages decided to do this in order to protect their students from misusing the powers of these mantras. In order to unlock their power, one

would need to be initiated into them. This is the case with the
Gayatri mantra and the Mahamryutunjaya mantras as well
as number of others.

Obstacles to Higher Consciousness and Remedies

There are three afflictions that hinder the aspiring soul during its
journey of spiritual development. These are mala, vikshepa and
avarana.

- Mala means impurity, physical as well as mental

- Vikshepa are the internal and external disturbances that
  plague us

- Avarana is the curtain of "not knowing" that clouds our
  consciousness – it is our basic ignorance

There is an allegory to illustrate our condition: A coin lies on the
bottom of a bowl filled with water. If the water is dirty (mala),
also turbulent (vikshepa) and, on top of that, is covered by a cloth
(avarana) we cannot see the coin at the bottom of the vessel.
Steps taken in isolation do not help. If we only remove the cloth
our vision will still be obstructed by the waves. And even if the
waves subside we are still unable to discern the coin because the

water is polluted and cloudy. Then what to do? All three obstacles must be removed. Firstly we must take the cloth away, then filter and purify the water, and lastly quieten the waves. Then the coin can be seen clearly and raised to the surface.

Mala are our impure thoughts. They obscure and darken our mind. We are mistaken if we think that no-one can read our thoughts. We know exactly what we are thinking. "Freedom of thought" is our birthright, but we should not forget that every thought, as well as every action, comes back to us as karma.

External dirt is simple to remove, but inner impurities stick in the depths of our consciousness and are not so easily disposed of. To purify our body we need very little time – less than an hour, but we may require several lifetimes to purify our consciousness.

Vikshepa are disturbances that can stem either from the outer world or our inner world. We can protect ourselves and take precautions against external disturbances like noise, heat or cold. This is not the case with attacks from inside - such as fears and anxiety complexes. These are only prevented with difficulty. Nervousness, worry and annoyance are internal disturbances that churn up our mind and obstruct us until we are able to get to their root cause.

Hidden within us lie six very special abilities that help us overcome the influences of these barriers of mala, vikshepa and avarana. What are these assets that we can cultivate? To discover them requires keen self-observation and training of the consciousness. First we must find out what prevents us from discovering these inner friends and helpers.

We are hampered by the four inner foes:

- Kama – passion

- Krodha – anger

- Moha – delusion

- Lobha – greed

Moha lays the foundation stone for kama, krodha and lobha. Delusion is the main cause of our mental, psychic or physical suffering and our attachments. It is the reason for depression, fear, jealousy and sadness. Attachment is always connected with fear. Even when we are happy in the present moment the fear of losing that which we believe is absolutely necessary for our happiness sits deeply within us. The attempt to safeguard and increase our possessions strengthens and nurtures passion and desire within us. The fear of loss leads subsequently to the eruption of anger, jealousy and hostility.

Naturally we should look after and care about our possessions. Certainly we should love and take care of our children, partner and friends. But, it is important to respect the freedom of everyone - to make nobody dependent upon us, and also not to become dependent upon anyone. Attachment is like a spider's web that holds us firmly and stifles us. It is not my intent to say that we are not allowed to own things or we should leave our family and friends. On the contrary! I wish everyone a prosperous and happy life - but we should not forget that after death we cannot take even one coin with us, and that all worldly relationships are temporary.

Through the practice of Yoga and following ethical principles we are able to purify the four antahkaranas (mind, consciousness, intellect and ego), to overcome false attachments and the other qualities mentioned above, and to transform their destructive energy into the good. We can then cultivate and develop the six treasures that can help us overcome the four inner foes and the three fundamental afflictions.

The six attributes that we need to cultivate as antidotes are:

- Shama

- Dama

- Sharaddha

- Titiksha

- Uparati

- Samadhana

Shama is inner silence and calmness. It is peace! We achieve this as we withdraw the mind and senses from the bustle of the external world and focus on the inner Self – this is enabled by the practice of pratyahara during our yogic practice.

Dama means self-control. When we rein in the senses, thoughts and emotions with the higher mind (buddhi), so that they do not gallop away like wild horses, we are able to avoid ill-considered actions and spare ourselves from the ensuing problems and suffering.

Sharaddha is faith. It is a trust - something that is absolutely fundamental to spiritual as well as all worldly relationships. Where trust is missing, doubt grows and gradually destroys love. Doubt is like 'sand in a salad'. A salad that has grains of sand mixed in with it is inedible, even though it may still appear to be delicious. Therefore remove your doubts and begin to trust. However, be careful to vet the truth of falsehoods before you place your faith.

Who should you trust? We should have faith in ourselves first of all. Many people have lost their self-confidence. Through the rediscovery of your inner treasures you also regain your self-confidence.

Next, have faith in your path and your purpose so that nothing or no-one can undermine it or dissuade you in any way. The way to perfection requires unconditional trust. Once you have decided upon a path, do not allow yourself to be discouraged by difficulties. Be deeply committed to the attainment of what you have resolved to do, and say to yourself with inner certainty: 'I will make it.' Do not think 'I will try it' - with this type of thinking you cripple yourself. Courageously seize the opportunities that fate offers you and place the outcome of your efforts in the hands of the Divine.

Thirdly, have absolute faith in your Master – whether he or she is an internal guide or manifested externally. If you constantly doubt, then you are unable to see the truth even if it is directly before your eyes. Shraddha is primal trust, such as that between a mother and her child. A baby stops crying as soon as the mother takes it in her arms because it feels safe and secure. Whoever possesses this natural capacity to trust is happy and successful in life. You are only able to recognize the truth when you show unconditional trust in the Master, just like a child to its mother.

Uparati means to rise above things by not being dependent or being afraid. When you face everything with a positive attitude you cannot really be harmed because you are able to draw valuable lessons from everything, even accidents. Fear and problems always arise when we are afraid of losing something. A wealthy person who is surrounded by guards, bolts and padlocks is, in reality, a prisoner of his possessions.

In the principles of Raja Yoga it is said: "You should not accumulate possessions." Rise above worldly things and practice renunciation – not as a painful turning away from the world, but as a liberating act of turning towards the Divine. Mahatma Gandhi also said: "Renounce and enjoy". This is an important

[161]

rule of life.

Titiksha is equanimity and inner strength. Everyone is aware that they will continue to face obstacles and difficulties in life. When was our existence ever completely free of problems? Don't give in to your fears even if a situation appears to be hopeless. Remember that nothing lasts forever. Only the Self is unchanging and eternal. Everything else is changeable and transitory because time continues to march on inexorably. The body is changing every second - just as thoughts, feelings and situations also continue to change. Never give in to despair, even if bad things are happening to you. Pray for titiksha, inner strength, courage and steadfastness.

Samadhana means inner composure and is the ability to remain focused on one's goal. Never lose sight of the goal. If disturbances and resistance surface, sit yourself down quietly, close your eyes and carefully think about the situation. If you feel a surge of malice or rage building within you do not act at once. **Remain detached and merely observe your emotions**. A great saint said: "When the waves are high one should not dive into the sea for pearls." Therefore wait until the inner waves have subsided, and then carefully and calmly ask yourself:

- What have I done? – Why have I acted so?

- What have I thought? – Why have I thought so?

- What do I think now? – Why do I think so?

- What should I think? – How should I act?

Further inquire of yourself:

- How important was it?

- Why was it so important?

Or, thinking more deeply,

- Was it at all important?

- What have I lost?

- Have I really lost anything?

- Was it of importance for my eternal happiness?

- You can never lose what is important for eternal happiness - therefore, in reality you have lost nothing.

The second aspect of samadhana is to reflect on the sense and reason for existence:

- Who has created this world and for what purpose?

- Where do I come from and where do I go to?

- What is reality and what is unreality?

- What is my purpose in life?

Therefore, on a general level, samadhana means to withdraw and observe. When the inner waves have subsided we can dive deeply within ourselves. Only in this way are we able to recognize the truth, the reality, and understand the sense of all difficulties and suffering. When we are able to withdraw the mind from external things, we can connect with the higher consciousness within ourselves and know the answers to all our questions.

Rudra Shivananda

Conclusion

It is my sincere hope that this small work on the great path of Mantra Yoga will help those who are pursuing this path or thinking about taking this path. Obviously, it is no substitute for a living guide, but should help to put the practice in proper perspective so as to inspire rather those who may have begun to have doubts about their mantra sadhana.

I feel that the practice of Level 1 mantras are very important to set the right mind-frame for further practice. My advice is to take your time and not jumb right into Level 2 practice until you feel the impact of the Level 1 mantras - a peaceful and alert mind focussed on positive thoughts.

For the best results, the practice of Level 3 should be only done with initiation into the chosen mantra.

Om Shanti, Shanti, Shanti!

Appendix

An exposition on mantras would be incomplete without some discussion about Yantras. These are visual tools that serve in meditation either as centering devices or as symbolic compositions of the energy pattern of a deity as perceived by adepts. For religious or material purposes, yantras are the geometric designs imprinted on a copper or silver plate or even as multi-colored inks on paper. They comprise ancient sacred symbols manifested by the ancient seers and later combined together by yogis and adepts as devices for devotional sadhanas or practices, and as objects to direct our mind and worship - tools for mental concentration and meditation. Other yantras were formulated for their material benefits - keeping a specific yantra in a particular direction in the home, and worshiping is said to have distinct auspicious effects. Yet other yantras formulated for the planetary forces serve to offset astrological effects due to past karma.

For our purpose of spiritual evolution, it is not necessary to invoke the use of yantras – mantras can function solely by their own power. In contrast, yantras are mere dead symbols or metal plates without the proper invocation of the correct mantra to infuse energy and life into it.

Just as there is a difference between mind and body, so there is between mantra and yantra. Yantra is the body or form of a specific universal power and mantra is the mind, consciousness, spirit or name. Yantra is the external, visual expression through which the power can express itself.
When a yantra is used for worship and the energy is invoked in it, it becomes a symbolic representative of the deity and actually it becomes the deity when the person abandons his analytical,

critical attitude and the energy circulates in higher centers. Every yantra becomes the dwelling place of the deity it represents. No murti (statuary) or picture of a deity is as powerful as a yantra in meditation, because it is composed of archetypical forms that are common to all existing phenomena. The very process of making a yantra is an archetypical activity that works with the encoding of the genes. During the process one moves from concrete reality to abstract truth.

The Sanskrit word yantra comes from the root 'yam', which means supporting or holding the essence of an object or concept. The syllable 'tra' comes from "trana" or liberation from bondage. Therefore yantra can mean liberation from the cycle of birth and rebirth (moksha). As a tool, yantra meditation is used to withdraw consciousness from the outer world, so as to help the student to go beyond the normal framework of mind to higher states of consciousness.

Drawing and painting yantras teaches the mind how to concentrate, how to be one-pointed. To some people this practice of painting yantras is fascinating and absorbing, while others might not find it as interesting as doing calligraphy or singing, but creating a yantra is a good preliminary to meditation. The geometrical forms of the yantra activate the right hemisphere, which is visual and nonverbal.

Most people are nowadays more left hemisphere dominated and are deficient in right hemisphere education which causes some loss of imagination and of faith in higher values. This dichotomy of the hemispheres causes stress and unhappiness. Right hemisphere education through art, dance and music is needed to restore the balance. By coloring and drawing the geometrical yantra diagrams, based on the vision of the sages, we can make both our hemispheres work simultaneously and calmly, to achieve faith and live in constant awareness.

Symbols used in yantras

A black point on a white background forms the most precise and powerful yantra for meditation. But it is too simple to say that a yantra is a point on a surface which serves as a field for gazing. The point (bindu) is the center of the yantra. It signifies unity, the origin, the principle of manifestation and emanation. Although in theory a true point has no magnitude, but to have a point in concrete form, it is given the smallest practicable magnitude. This point is the first step in visualizing the abstract, the form-less. Meditation or concentration on this point brings the mind towards abstract concentration which is used as a means to Self-realization.

A circle is an extension of a point. With the radius of desire, the point draws a circle around itself and expands. However, the circle also creates an individual consciousness out of cosmic consciousness. After the point and the circle the triangle is the simplest yantra form. Upward triangles draw the attention up and away from the world, while a downward triangle moves towards the material world.

The shatkona (Sanskrit name for the symbol of the six-pointed star) is composed of a balance between:
- An upwards triangle denoting action (or service), extroversion, masculinity or Shiva
- A downwards triangle denoting introversion, meditativeness, goddess energy or Shakti

Other complex symbols include:
- The lotus flower typically represent chakras, with each petal representing a psychic propensity (or vritti) associated

---

with that chakra.
- A swastika represents good luck, welfare, prosperity or spiritual victory
- Bija mantras (usually represented as characters of Devanagari (Sanskrit or Hindi alphabet) that correspond to the acoustic roots of a particular chakra or vritti)

Astrological yantras are used in working with the energy of the nine planets. Numerical yantras are not composed of basic geometrical forms but of numbers. Some of these yantras are used as talismans. When working with a yantra, a mantra is needed to invoke the vital life force (prana) of the particular deity.

Important Yantras

Shree Yantra

This is by tradition one of the most auspicious, important and powerful yantras – giving not only the maximum benefit, but can be used by everyone regardless of station in life. It is the source of attaining all worldly desires & fulfilling all wishes through inner cosmic power and mental strength. 'Shree' signifies success and wealth and 'Yantra' as the means or an instrument. Therefore it is the 'instrument for success and wealth.'

Shree Yantra has that mystical power to fulfill all our wishes and change our life for the better. It is said that any person using it achieves peace, harmony and his or her heart's desires.

The sacred geometry of the Shree Yantra clears away all negative energies - the karmic fog that surrounds our lives - standing in the way of peace, prosperity and harmony

Rudra Shivananda

Figure 23
Shree Yantra

Shree Yantra can be seen in either two dimension form - nine intertwined isosceles triangles. This form is especially useful for meditation. In the three dimension form, it is a multistep pyramid – the meru cosmic grid signifying unlimited abundance and positive powers. This multi -pyramidal geometry has seven steps and forty-three petals with a base angle of 51.50 degrees.

The Shree Yantra can be formed with different materials. The best material is crystal – it balances and harmonizes the aura around us and removes the negative energy. It is commonly placed in the home or office to purify the place by the power of crystal and the mystical geometry.

[170]

Shri Mahamrityunjaya Yantra

This yantra protects one from destructive influences like accidents, crises, sickness, epidemic, and similar life-threatening calamities. It promotes a long-life.

Figure 24
Mahamrityunjaya Yantra

Surya Yantra

It promotes good health and well-being, protects one from diseases and promotes intellect.

Panchadashi Yantra

This yantra has the blessings of Lord Shiva and ensures morality, wealth, family happiness, and salvation.

Durga Yantra
This overcomes all karmic obstacles and destroys negativity.

Figure 24
Durga Yantra

Note: it is quite powerful to use the yantra together with the appropriate mantra. It becomes insightful meditation if done with spiritual intent or a strong manifesting vehicle when done for a material purpose. There is usually strict procedures that must be learned and followed for such uses.

A universal form of yantra meditation

The following meditation can be used for any two dimensional yantra.

Looking at the yantra, allow your eyes to focus on its center. This dot in the center is called the bindu, which represents the unity that underlies all the diversity of the physical world.

Now allow your eyes to see the triangle that encloses the bindu. The downward pointing triangle represents the feminine creative power, while the upward facing triangle represents male energy. Allow your vision to expand to include the circles outside of the triangles. They represent the cycles of cosmic rhythms. The image of the circle embodies the notion that time has no beginning and no end. The farthest region of space and the innermost nucleus of an atom both pulsate with the same rhythmic energy of creation. That rhythm is within you and without you.

Bring your awareness to lotus petals outside the circle. Notice that they are pointing outwards, as if opening. They illustrate the unfolding of our understanding. The lotus also represents the heart, the seat of the Self. When the heart opens, understanding comes.

The square at the outside of the yantra represents the world of form, the material world that our senses show us, the illusion of separateness, of well-defined edges and boundaries. At the periphery of the figure are four T-shaped portals, or gateways. Notice that they point toward the interior of the yantra, the inner spaces of life. They represent our earthly passage from the external and material to the internal and sacred.

Now take a moment to gaze into the yantra, letting the different shapes and patterns emerge naturally, allowing your eyes to be held loosely in focus. Gaze at the center of the yantra on the page. Without moving your eyes, gradually begin to expand your field of vision. Continue expanding your vision until you are taking in information from greater than 180 degrees. Notice that all this information was there all along, you just became aware of it. Now slowly reverse the process by re-focusing back to the center of the yantra. Now gently close your eyes. You may still see the yantra in your mind's eye. The patterns of creativity represented by these primordial shapes express the fundamental forces of nature. They govern the world and they govern you.

Specific meditation for Shree Yantra

The following meditation expands consciousness and induces calm. It also integrates the masculine and feminine aspects of our being as well as balancing the two brain hemispheres. All this can be done in as little as five minutes.

Before reading any further, take 5 minutes to look at the very center of this Sri Yantra image. Don't strain your eyes, but try not to blink if you can. So without any strain keep watching the dot in the middle, and allow yourself to become aware of the whole image whilst being focused on the dot.

You may start seeing the lines as though dancing with different shapes and patterns emerging and the whole image moving. As these things are happening, your brain is getting more harmonious, your masculine and feminine sides are merging. You will start to vibrate at a higher frequency and your whole body is bathed in the energy of harmony.

When you finish gazing at the yantra, close your eyes and see it further evolving in your mind's eye.

The Symbolism of Shree Yantra

In the lines and curves of Shree Yantra (also called "Shree Chakra") the whole existence is depicted. From these lines emerges the Universe.

It contains the Golden Ratio and the five elements of the Universe – Earth, Fire, Water, Air and Ether.

The dot in the center represents the big bang as we call it, the point from which the entire creation sprang. It also represents the unity that underlies all the diversity we see in the Universe. The dot is the element of ether in the yantra.

The triangles represent male and female energies whose interaction sustains Maya (the phenomenal world). Maya dances in forms and shapes until the spiritual seeker decides to turn the gaze inwards.

The downward-pointing triangles are female and represent the water element. The upward pointing ones are male, and represent the fire element.

The circle enclosing triangles represents the cycles of our existence, as well as time, which, like a circle, has no beginning or end.

The lotus petals represent the unfolding of knowledge as well as the heart chakra. When the heart chakra opens, we naturally become open to higher truths, and our knowledge blossoms like the lotus petal. Lotus represents all five elements of the universe: Ether, Air, Water, Fire and Earth.

The square represents our physical world and therefore is of the element of Earth. Each square wall has an opening, which is a portal into the Inner World, leading you to the very cause of creation – the central point, called 'bindu' in yogic cosmology. There are four T-shaped portals in total, as you can see in the image.
Sri Yantra is the symbol of cosmic perfection, so focusing on it brings more beauty and harmony into your inner and outer worlds. It's a visual symbol of a primordial sound OM

.

The center point is the very start of Maya. It's the explosion of the Divine into being. This smallest dot sustains the Maya, and if it were to move even slightly to any direction, the whole reality would collapse.

Glossary

Acharya a preceptor, spiritual instructor; also guru

Advaita ("nonduality"): the truth and teaching that there is only One Reality (*Atman, Brahman*), especially as found in the Upanishads

Ahamkara ("I-maker"): the individuation principle, or ego, which must be transcended

Ahimsa ("nonharming"): one of the five important moral disciplines (*yama*)

Ajapa mantra ("unpronounced mantra"): the sound *hamsa* made by the breath around 21600 times per day

Akasha ("ether/space"): the first of the five material elements of which the physical universe is composed; also used to designate "inner" space, that is, the space of consciousness (called *cid-akasha*)

Amrita ("immortal/immortality"): a designation of the deathless Spirit (*atman, purusha*); also the nectar of immortality that oozes from the psycho-energetic center at the crown of the head (see *sahasrara-chakra*) when it is activated and transforms the body into a "divine body" (*divya-deha*)

Ananda ("bliss"): the condition of utter joy, which is an essential quality of the ultimate Reality

Anga ("limb"): a fundamental category of the yogic path, such as *yama, niyama, asana, dharana, dhyana, pranayama, pratyahara,* *samadhi,*

Antakharana ("inner instrument"): consists of higher mind (buddhi) ego (ahamkara), lower mind (manas)

Asana ("seat"): a physical posture (see also *anga*); the third limb (*anga*) of Patanjali's eightfold path; originally this meant only a meditation posture, but subsequently, in hatha yoga, this aspect of the yogic path was greatly developed

Ashrama ("that where effort is made"): a hermitage; also a stage of life, such as *brahmacharya*, householder, forest dweller, and complete renouncer (*sannyasin*)

Ashta-anga-yoga, ashtanga-yoga ("eight-limbed union"): the eightfold yoga of Patanjali, consisting of moral discipline (*yama*), self-restraint (*niyama*), posture (*asana*), breath control (*pranayama*), sensory inhibition (*pratyahara*), concentration (*dharana*), meditation (*dhyana*), and ecstasy (*samadhi*), leading to liberation (*kaivalya*)

Asmita ("I-am-ness"): a concept of Patanjali's eight-limbed yoga, roughly synonymous with *ahamkara*

Atman ("self"): the transcendental Self, or Spirit, which is eternal and super-conscious; our true nature or identity; sometimes a distinction is made between the *atman* as the individual self and the *parama-atman* as the transcendental Self

Avidya ("ignorance"): the root cause of suffering (*duhkha*)

Bandha ("bond/bondage"): the fact that human beings are typically bound by ignorance (*avidya*), which causes them to lead a life governed by karmic habit rather than inner freedom generated through wisdom (*vidya, jnana*)

Bhakta ("devotee"): a disciple practicing bhakti yoga

[179]

Bhakti ("devotion/love"): the love of the bhakta toward the Divine or the guru as a manifestation of the Divine; also the love of the Divine toward the devotee

Bhakti Yoga ("Yoga of devotion"): a major branch of the yoga tradition, utilizing the feeling capacity to connect with the ultimate Reality conceived as a supreme Person

Bindu ("seed/point"): the creative potency of anything where all energies are focused; the dot (also called *tilaka*) worn on the forehead as indicative of the third eye; also an intrinsic part of a mantra

Brahma ("he who has grown expansive"): the Creator of the universe, the first principle (*tattva*) to emerge out of the ultimate Reality (*brahman*)

Brahmacharya (from *brahma* and *acarya* "brahmic conduct"): the discipline of chastity, which produces *ojas*

Brahman ("that which has grown expansive"): the ultimate Reality

Buddha ("awakened"): a designation of the person who has attained enlightenment (*bodhi*) and therefore inner freedom; honorific title of Gautama, the founder of Buddhism, who lived in the sixth century B.C.E.

Buddhi ("she who is conscious, awake"): the higher mind, which is the seat of wisdom (*vidya, jnana*)

Chakra ("wheel"): literally, the wheel of a wagon; metaphorically, one of the psycho-energetic centers of the subtle body (*sukshma-sharira*); in Buddhist yoga, five such centers are known, while in Hindu yoga often seven or more such centers are mentioned: *mula-adhara-cakra (muladhara-cakra)* at the base of the spine, *svadhishthana-cakra* at the genitals, *manipura-cakra* at the navel, *anahata-cakra* at the heart, *vishuddha-cakra* or *vishuddhi-cakra* at the throat, *ajna-cakra* in the middle of the head, and *sahasrara-cakra* at the top of the head

Chin-mudra ("consciousness seal"): a common hand gesture (*mudra*) in meditation (*dhyana*), which is formed by bringing the tips of the index finger and the thumb together, while the remaining fingers are kept straight

Cit ("consciousness"): the super-conscious ultimate Reality

Citta ("that which is conscious"): ordinary consciousness, the mind, as opposed to *cit*

Darshana ("seeing"): vision in the literal and metaphorical sense; a system of philosophy, such as the *yoga-darshana* of Patanjali

Deva ("he who is shining"): a male deity, such as Shiva, Vishnu, or Krishna, either in the sense of the ultimate Reality or a high angelic being

Devi ("she who is shining"): a female deity such as Parvati, Lakshmi, or Radha, either in the sense of the ultimate Reality (in its feminine pole) or a high angelic being

Dharana ("holding"): concentration, the sixth limb (*anga*) of Patanjali's eight-limbed yoga

Dharma ("bearer"): a term of numerous meanings; often used in the sense of "law," "lawfulness," "virtue," "righteousness," "norm"

Dhyana ("ideating"): meditation, the seventh limb (*anga*) of Patanjali's eight-limbed yoga

Diksha ("initiation"): the act and condition of induction into the hidden aspects of yoga or a particular lineage of teachers; all traditional yoga is initiatory

Duhkha ("bad axle space"): suffering, a fundamental fact of life, caused by ignorance (*avidya*) of our true nature (i.e., the Self or *atman*)

Gayatri-mantra: a famous Vedic *mantra* recited particularly at sunrise: *tat savitur varenyam bhargo devasya dhimahi dhiyo yo nah pracodayat*

Granthi ("knot"): any one of three common blockages in the central pathway (*sushumna-nadi*) preventing the full ascent of the serpent power (*kundalini-shakti*); the three knots are known as *brahma-granthi* (at the lowest psycho-energetic center of the subtle body), the *vishnu-granthi* (at the heart), and the *rudra-granthi* (at the eyebrow center)

Guna ("quality"): a term that has numerous meanings, including "virtue"; often refers to any of the three primary "qualities" or constituents of nature (*prakriti*): *tamas* (the principle of inertia), *rajas* (the dynamic principle), and *sattva* (the principle of lucidity)

Guru ("he who is heavy, weighty"): a spiritual teacher

Guru-Yoga ("Yoga [relating to] the teacher"): a yogic approach that makes the guru the fulcrum of a disciple's practice; all traditional forms of yoga contain a strong element of guru-yoga

Hamsa ("swan/gander"): apart from the literal meaning, this term also refers to the breath (*prana*) as it moves within the body; the individuated consciousness (*jiva*) propelled by the breath; see *jiva-atman*; also to the liberated soul

Hatha Yoga ("Forceful Yoga"): a major branch of yoga, developed by Gorakshanath and other adepts c. 1000 C.E., and emphasizing the physical aspects of the transformative path, notably postures (*asana*) and cleansing techniques (*shodhana*), but also breath control (*pranayama*)

Ida-nadi ("pale conduit"): the *prana* current or arc ascending on the left side of the central channel (*sushumna nadi*) associated with the parasympathetic nervous system and having a cooling or calming effect on the mind when activated

Ishvara ("ruler"): the Lord; referring either to the Creator (see *Brahma*) or, in Patanjali's yoga-darshana, to a special transcendental Self (*purusha*)

Ishvara-pranidhana ("dedication to the Lord"): in Patanjali's eight-limbed yoga one of the practices of self-restraint (*niyama*)

Japa ("muttering"): the recitation of *mantras*

Jiva-atman, jivatman ("individual self"): the individuated consciousness, as opposed to the ultimate Self (*parama-atman*)

Jivan-mukta ("he who is liberated while alive"): an adept who, while still embodied, has attained liberation (*moksha*)

Jivan-mukti ("living liberation"): the state of liberation while being embodied

Jnana ("knowledge/wisdom"): both worldly knowledge or world-transcending wisdom, depending on the context; see also *prajna*; cf. *avidya*

Jnana-Yoga ("Yoga of wisdom"): the path to liberation based on wisdom, or the direct intuition of the transcendental Self (*atman*) through the steady application of discernment between the Real and the unreal and renunciation of what has been identified as unreal (or inconsequential to the achievement of liberation)

Kaivalya ("isolation"): the state of absolute freedom from conditioned existence, as explained in *ashta-anga-yoga*; in the non-dualistic (*advaita*) traditions of India, this is usually called *moksha* or *mukti* (meaning "release" from the fetters of ignorance, or *avidya*)

Kali: a Goddess embodying the fierce (dissolving) aspect of the Divine

Kali-yuga: the dark age of spiritual and moral decline, said to be current now; here, kali does not refer to the Goddess Kali but to the losing throw of a die

Kama ("desire"): the appetite for sensual pleasure blocking the path to true bliss (*ananda*); the only desire conducive to freedom is the impulse toward liberation, called *mumukshutva*

Karman, karma ("action"): activity of any kind, including ritual acts; said to be binding only so long as engaged in a self-centered way; the "karmic" consequence of one's actions; destiny

Karma Yoga ("Yoga of action"): the liberating path of self-transcending action

Karuna ("compassion"): universal sympathy; in Buddhist yoga the complement of wisdom (*prajna*)

Kosha ("casing"): any one of five "envelopes" surrounding the transcendental Self (*atman*) and thus blocking its light: *anna-maya-kosha* ("envelope made of food," the physical body), *prana-maya-kosha* ("envelope made of life force"), *mano-maya-kosha* ("envelope made of mind"), *vijnana-maya-kosha* ("envelope made of consciousness"), and *ananda-maya-kosha* ("envelope made of bliss")

Krishna ("Puller"): an incarnation of God Vishnu, the God-man whose teachings can be found in the Bhagavad Gita and the Bhagavata-Purana

Kundalini-shakti ("coiled power"): according to Tantra and hatha yoga, the serpent power or spiritual energy, which exists in potential form at the lowest psycho-energetic center of the body (i.e., the *mula-adhara-cakra*) and which must be awakened and guided to the center at the crown (i.e., the *sahasrara-cakra*) for full enlightenment to occur

Kundalini-Yoga: the yogic path focusing on the *kundalini* process as a means of liberation

Laya Yoga ("Yoga of dissolution"): an advanced form or process of Tantric yoga by which the energies associated with the various psycho-energetic centers (*cakra*) of the subtle body are gradually dissolved through the ascent of the serpent power (*kundalini-shakti*)

Linga ("mark"): the phallus as a principle of creativity; a symbol of God Shiva

Mahatma (from maha-atman, "great self"): an honorific title (meaning something like "a great soul") bestowed on particularly meritorious individuals, such as Gandhi

Manas ("mind"): the lower mind, which is bound to the senses and yields information (*vijnana*) rather than wisdom (*jnana, vidya*)

Mantra (from the verbal root *man* "to think"): a sacred sound or phrase, such as *om, hum*, or *om namah shivaya*, that has a transformative effect on the mind of the individual reciting it; to be ultimately effective, a mantra needs to be given in an initiatory context (*diksha*)

Mantra-Yoga: the yogic path utilizing *mantras* as the primary means of liberation

Maya ("she who measures"): the deluding or illusive power of the world; illusion by which the world is seen as separate from the ultimate singular Reality (*atman*)

Moksha ("release"): the condition of freedom from ignorance (*avidya*) and the binding effect of *karma*; also called *mukti, kaivalya*

Mudra ("seal"): a hand gesture (such as *chin-mudra*) or whole-body gesture (such as *viparita-karani-mudra*); also a designation of the feminine partner in the Tantric sexual ritual

Nada ("sound"): the inner sound, as it can be heard through the practice of nada yoga or kundalini yoga

Nada-Yoga ("Yoga of the [inner] sound"): the yoga or process of producing and intently listening to the inner sound as a means of concentration and ecstatic self-transcendence

Nadi ("conduit"): one of 72,000 or more subtle channels along or through which the life force (*prana*) circulates, of which the three most important ones are the *ida-nadi, pingala-nadi,* and *sushumna-nadi*

Nadi-shodhana ("channel cleansing"): the practice of purifying the conduits, especially by means of breath control (*pranayama*)

Natha ("lord"): appellation of many North Indian masters of yoga, in particular adepts of the Kanphata ("Split-ear") school founded by Gorakshanath

Nirodha ("restriction"): in Patanjali's eight-limbed yoga, the very basis of the process of concentration, meditation, and ecstasy; in the first instance, the restriction of the "whirls of the mind" (*citta-vritti*)

Niyama ("[self-restraint"): the second limb of Patanjali's eightfold path, which consists of purity (*saucha*), contentment (*samtosha*), austerity (*tapas*), study (*svadhyaya*), and dedication to the Lord (*ishvara-pranidhana*)

Nyasa ("placing"): the Tantric practice of infusing various body parts with life force (*prana*) by touching or thinking of the respective physical area; also part of mantra sadhana

Ojas ("vitality"): the subtle energy produced through practice, especially the discipline of chastity (*brahmacharya*)

Om: the original mantra symbolizing the ultimate Reality, which is prefixed to many mantric utterances

Parama-atman or *paramatman* ("supreme self"): the transcendental Self, which is singular, as opposed to the individuated self (*jiva-atman*) that exists in countless numbers in the form of living beings

Paramahamsa, *paramahansa* ("supreme swan"): an honorific title given to great adepts, such as Ramakrishna and Yogananda

Patanjali: a great yogi, the author or compiler of the Yoga Sutra, who lived c. 200 B.C.E.

Pingala-nadi ("reddish conduit"): the prana current or arc ascending on the right side of the central channel (*sushumna-nadi*) and associated with the sympathetic nervous system and having an energizing effect on the mind when activated; cf. *ida-nadi*

Prajna ("wisdom"): the opposite of spiritual ignorance (*ajnana, avidya*); one of two means of liberation in Buddhist yoga, the other being skillful means (*upaya*), i.e., compassion (*karuna*)

Prakriti ("creatrix"): nature, which is multilevel and, according to Patanjali's *yoga-darshana*, consists of an eternal dimension (called *pradhana* or "foundation"), levels of subtle existence (called *sukshma-parvan*), and the physical or coarse realm (called *sthula-parvan*); all of nature is deemed unconscious (*acit*), and therefore it is viewed as being in opposition to the transcendental Self or Spirit (*purusha*)

Prakriti-laya ("merging into Nature"): a high-level state of existence that falls short of actual liberation (*kaivalya*); the being who has attained that state

Prana ("life/breath"): life in general; the life force sustaining the body; the breath as an external manifestation of the subtle life force

Pranayama (from *prana* and *ayama*, "life/breath extension"): breath control, the fourth limb (*anga*) of Patanjali's eigthfold path, consisting of conscious inhalation (*puraka*) retention (*kumbhaka*) and exhalation (*recaka*); at an advanced state, breath retention occurs spontaneously for longer periods of time

Prasada ("grace/clarity"): divine grace; mental clarity

Pratyahara ("withdrawal"): sensory inhibition, the fifth limb (*anga*) of Patanjali's eightfold path

Puja ("worship"): ritual worship, which is an important aspect of many forms of yoga, notably bhakti yoga and Tantra

Purana ("Ancient [History]"): a type of popular encyclopedia dealing with royal genealogy, cosmology, philosophy, and ritual; there are eighteen major and many more minor works of this nature

Purusha ("male"): the transcendental Self (*atman*) or Spirit, a designation that is mostly used in Samkhya and Patanjali's *yoga-darshana*

Raja-Yoga ("Royal Yoga"): a late medieval designation of Patanjali's eightfold *yoga-darshana*, also known as classical yoga

Rama: an incarnation of God Vishnu preceding Krishna; the principal hero of the *Ramayana*

Rig-Veda : the oldest part of the pre-historic scriptures of the Eternal Dharma passed down orally through countless generations

Rishi ("seer"): a category of Vedic sage; an honorific title of certain venerated masters, such as the Markendeya , the seer of the Mahamryutunjaya mantra

Sadhana ("accomplishing"): spiritual discipline leading to siddhi ("perfection" or "accomplishment")

Sahaja ("together born"): a medieval term denoting the fact that the transcendental Reality and the empirical reality are not truly separate but coexist, or with the latter being an aspect or misperception of the former; often rendered as "spontaneous" or "spontaneity"; the *sahaja* state is the natural condition, that is, enlightenment or realization

Samadhi ("putting together"): the ecstatic or unitive state in which the meditator becomes one with the object of meditation, the eighth and final limb (*anga*) of Patanjali's eightfold path; there are many types of *samadhi*, the most significant distinction being between *samprajnata* (conscious) and *asamprajnata* (supraconscious) ecstasy; only the latter leads to the dissolution of the karmic factors deep within the mind; beyond both types of ecstasy is enlightenment, which is also sometimes called *sahaja-samadhi* or the condition of "natural" or "spontaneous" ecstasy, where there is perfect continuity of super-conscious throughout waking, dreaming, and sleeping

Samkhya ("Number"): one of the main traditions of Hinduism, which is concerned with the classification of the principles (*tattva*) of existence and their proper discernment in order to distinguish between Spirit (*purusha*) and the various aspects of Nature (*prakriti*); this influential system grew out of the ancient (pre-Buddhist) Samkhya-Yoga tradition and was codified in the *Samkhya-Karika* of Ishvara Krishna (c. 350 C.E.)

Samprajnata-samadhi; see *samadhi*

Samsara ("confluence"): the finite world of change, as opposed to the ultimate Reality (*brahman* or *nirvana*)

Samskara ("activator"): the subconscious impression left behind by each act of volition, which, in turn, leads to renewed psycho-mental activity; the countless *samskaras* hidden in the depth of the mind are ultimately eliminated only in *asamprajnata-samadhi* (see *samadhi*)

Samyama ("constraint"): the combined practice of concentration (*dharana*), meditation (*dhyana*), and ecstasy (*samadhi*) in regard to the same object

Sannyasa ("casting off"): the state of renunciation, which is the fourth and final stage of life *(see ashrama)* and consisting primarily in an inner turning away from what is understood to be finite and secondarily in an external letting go of finite things

Sannyasin ("he who has cast off"): a renouncer

Sat ("being/reality/truth"): the ultimate Reality (*atman* or *brahman*)

Sat-sanga ("true company/company of Truth"): the practice of frequenting the good company of saints, sages, Self-realized adepts, and their disciples, in whose company the ultimate Reality can be felt more palpably

Satya ("truth/truthfulness"): truth, a designation of the ultimate Reality; also the practice of truthfulness, which is an aspect of moral discipline (*yama*)

Shakti ("power"): the ultimate Reality in its feminine aspect, or the power pole of the Divine

Shakti-pata ("descent of power"): the process of initiation, or spiritual baptism, by means of the benign transmission of an advanced or even enlightened adept (*siddha*), which awakens the *shakti* within a disciple, thereby initiating or enhancing the process of liberation

Shankara ("He who is benevolent"): the eighth-century adept who was the greatest proponent of non-dualism (Advaita Vedanta) and whose philosophical school was probably responsible for the decline of Buddhism in India

Shishya ("student/disciple"): the initiated disciple of a guru

Shiva ("He who is benign"): the Divine; a deity that has served yogins as an archetypal model throughout the ages

Shodhana ("cleansing/purification"): a fundamental aspect of all yogic paths; a category of purification practices in hatha yoga

Shraddha ("faith"): an essential disposition on the yogic path, which must be distinguished from mere belief

Shuddhi ("purification/purity"): the state of purity; a synonym of *shodhana*

Siddha ("accomplished"): an adept of Yoga and Tantra; if fully Self-realized, the designation *maha-siddha* or "great adept" is often used

Siddhi ("accomplishment/perfection"): spiritual perfection, the attainment of flawless identity with the ultimate Reality (*atman* or *brahman*); paranormal ability, of which the yoga tradition knows many kinds

Spanda ("vibration"): a key concept of Kashmir's Shaivism according to which the ultimate Reality itself "quivers," that is, is inherently creative rather than static (as conceived in Advaita Vedanta)

Sushumna-nadi ("very gracious channel"): the central *prana* current or arc in or along which the serpent power (*kundalini-shakti*) must ascend toward the psycho-energetic center (*chakra*) at the crown of the head in order to attain liberation (*moksha*)

Sutra ("thread"): an aphoristic statement; a work consisting of aphoristic statements, such as Patanjali's Yoga Sutra

Svadhyaya ("one's own going into"): study, an important aspect of the yogic path, listed among the practices of self-restraint (*niyama*) in Patanjali's eightfold yoga; the recitation of *mantras*

Tantra ("Loom"): a type of Sanskrit work containing Tantric teachings; the tradition of Tantrism, which focuses on the *shakti* side of spiritual life and which originated in the early post-Christian era and achieved its classical features around 1000 C.E.; Tantrism has a "right-hand" (*dakshina*) or conservative and a "left-hand" (*vama*) or unconventional branch, with the latter utilizing, among other things, sexual rituals

Tapas ("glow/heat"): austerity, penance, which is an ingredient of all yogic approaches, since they all involve self-transcendence

Tattva ("thatness"): a fact or reality; a particular category of existence such as the *ahamkara, buddhi, manas*; the ultimate Reality

Turiya ("fourth"), also called *cathurtha*: the transcendental

Reality, which exceeds the three conventional states of consciousness, namely waking, sleeping, and dreaming

Upanishad ("sitting near"): a type of scripture representing the concluding portion of the revealed literature of Sanatana Dharma, hence the designation Vedanta for the teachings of these sacred works

Upaya ("means"): in Buddhist yoga, the practice of compassion (*karuna*)

Vairagya ("dispassion"): the attitude of inner renunciation

Books by Rudra Shivananda

Chakra selfHealing by the Power of Om

Yoga of Purification and Transformation

Surya Yoga - Healing by Solar Power

Breathe Like Your Life Depends On It

In Light of Kriya Yoga

Healing Postures of the 18 Siddhas

Insight and Guidance for Spiritual Seekers

Practical Mantra Yoga

Breathe Better Live Longer

Nada: The Yoga of Inner Sound

website: www.rudrashivananda.com
blog: www.sanatanamitra.com
www.youtube.com/user/KriyaNathYogi

About the Author

Rudra Shivananda, a disciple of the Himalayan GrandMaster Yogiraj Siddhanath, is dedicated to the service of humanity through the furthering of human awareness and spiritual evolution. He teaches that the only lasting way to bring happiness into one's life is by a consistent practice of awareness and transformation. He has developed healing programs utilizing the energy centers [Chakras] and Prana Energy techniques through breath.

Rudra Shivananda is committed to spreading the message of the immortal Being called Babaji. He teaches the message of World and Individual Peace through the practice of Kriya Yoga. As a student and teacher of yoga for more than 40 years, he is trained as an Acharya or Spiritual Preceptor in the Indian Nath Tradition, closely associated with the Siddha tradition. He lives in the San Francisco Bay area, and has given initiations and workshops in USA, Ireland, England, Japan, Spain, Brazil, Russia, Singapore, Malaysia, Hong Kong, India, Australia, Canada and Estonia.

Rudra Shivananda

www.ingramcontent.com/pod-product-compliance
Lightning Source LLC
Chambersburg PA
CBHW062214080426
42734CB00010B/1883